"This is an excellent overview of the health care regulations with teeth. Things that are a normal way of doing business in other industries can cause a physician to lose their license and potentially be put in jail and out of business. As in house counsel for a medical practice "super-group", I am in the process of buying 200 copies of this book to distribute to all of my company's physician. This book can help them know when they should step back from an activity or situation that might get them in trouble.

- Bradley Brown, Vice President of Business Development, Anterro Health Systems, Miami, Florida

"I found this book to be very informative, easy to follow, and well organized on a very important topic."

- Daniel Sweeney, BayCare HomeCare Vice President, Clearwater, Florida

"This book brings home the importance of being able to understand some very complicated laws that have important purposes and implications for medical practices and medical practitioners. I highly recommend it to all of my colleagues.

- Kenneth B. Lee, D.O., Countryside Medical, Ocala, Florida

A PRACTICAL GUIDE TO ANTI-KICKBACK AND SELF-REFERRAL LAWS FOR PHYSICIANS

Lester J. Perling, J.D., M.H.A.
Broad and Cassel

Alan S. Gassman, J.D., LL.M.
Gassman Law Associates, P.A.

Printed in the United States of America.

ISBN-13: 978-1505827644
ISBN-10: 1505827647

DISCLAIMER OF WARRANTY AND LIMIT OF LIABILITY

The authors and publisher make no representations or warranties with respect to the accuracy of the contents of this work and do hereby specifically and expressly disclaim all warranties, including without limitation, warranties of title, merchantability, fitness for a particular purpose and non-infringement. No warranty may be created or extended by sales or promotional material associated with this work.

Any advice, strategies, and ideas contained herein may not be suitable for particular situations. This work is sold with the understanding that the publisher is not engaging in or rendering medical or legal advice or other professional services. If professional assistance is required, the services of a competent professional person should be sought.

Although the authors and publisher have made every effort to ensure that the information in this book was correct at press time, the authors and publisher do not assume and hereby disclaim any responsibility or liability whatsoever to the fullest extent allowed by law to any party for any and all direct, indirect, incidental, special, or consequential damages, or lost profits that result, either directly, or indirectly, from the use and application of any of the contents of this book. The purchaser or reader of this book alone assumes the risk for anything learned from this book.

This book is not intended as a substitute for legal advice and should not be used in such manner. Furthermore, the use of this book does not establish an attorney-client relationship.

The information provided in this book is designed for educational and informational purposes only and is not intended to serve as legal or medical advice.

References are provided for informational purposes only and do not constitute or imply endorsement, sponsorship, or recommendation of any websites or other sources. Readers should be aware that the websites listed in this book may change.

The views expressed herein are solely those of the authors and do not reflect the opinions of any other person or entity.

PREFACE

Lester Perling has been helping our practice understand and structure physician and medical practice arrangements for almost 20 years now. A multitude of rules will typically apply to a given proposed situation, and it has always been difficult to understand all of these rules.

I was therefore delighted when Lester agreed to join me in writing a definitive book on the subject that would enable physicians and advisors to understand and work within these complicated but often times logical rules and regulations.

Chapter 25 on The Biggest Mistakes That Doctors Make has received significant applause from the medical community.

Lester and I thank Kacie Hohnadell, a third year Stetson Law School student, for taking time from her busy schedule as Executive Editor at Stetson Law Review to pull together these materials and to make sure that our explanations are both understandable and properly cited.

Finally, we hope that you enjoy reading what we have put together here. I found it to be a great relief to finally have the actual rules "in one place" to reduce confusion and increase certainty in the complicated world that physicians find themselves in.

We welcome any and all questions, comments or suggestions that any reader may offer.

Alan S. Gassman, Esq.

TABLE OF CONTENTS

CHAPTER 1
INTRODUCTION

This book provides health care professionals, lawyers, medical office managers, and physician advisors with a straightforward explanation of the various federal laws controlling patient referrals and financial relationships involving medical practices, testing facilities, surgery centers, hospitals, and other businesses.[1]

Violation of these laws can lead to serious consequences, including civil monetary penalties, criminal penalties, denial of payment, and exclusion from participation in the federal healhcare program. Because the penalties for violating these laws are so severe, it is imperative that medical professionals be familiar with each of these rules and their prohibitions. While one law or safe harbor thereto may permit a particular action, another law will prevent the same act. Full comprehension of the law is vital to ensure that referrals, financial arrangements, and other actions comply with the relevant law. It is also advisable to have a compliance professional regularly review the medical practice's billing arrangements, compensation agreements, and patient referral procedures to assure that the highest degree of compliance is achieved.

The authors welcome any and all questions, comments, and suggestions, and will be updating this book in the future and sending notifications to readers who are on our mailing list. You can join our mailing list by sending an e-mail to Agassman@gassmanpa.com and/or Janine@gassmanpa.com.

This book provides an overview of the Federal laws addressing physician referrals and financial relationships, as well as some of the applicable administrative and judicial decisions. A brief summary of the laws discussed in this book is provided below:

FEDERAL LAWS

The federal Stark Law generally prohibits health care providers, including physicians in a group practice, from making referrals for "designated health services" covered by Medicare or Medicaid to an entity with which the physician or an immediate family member has a financial interest, unless a specific statutory exception is met.

The federal Anti-Kickback Statute imposes criminal penalties against any person who willfully pays, offers, solicits, or receives any "kickback" to induce the referral of items covered

1 The goal of this book is to provide physicians and other medical professionals with an overview of various laws governing the health care profession. This book only provides a summary of these laws and does not describe every requirement of the laws described herein. Although the authors have made every effort to ensure that the information contained in this book is accurate at press time, none of the material in this book should be taken or construed as legal advice. Before relying on information in this book, please consult an experienced health law attorney.

by Medicare or Medicaid. This law is broadly construed and can apply to any form of direct or indirect payment, such as giving away sports tickets or paying for dinners, unless a specific "safe harbor" applies.

These laws are not always clear in their intent or application, and we have pointed out a number of traps for the unwary using the following symbol:

CHAPTER 2
FEDERAL PHYSICIAN SELF-REFERRAL LAW (STARK LAW)

A. INTRODUCTION

The federal Physician Self-Referral Law, commonly referred to as the Stark Law, generally prohibits a physician from making referrals for "designated health services" covered by Medicare or Medicaid to an entity with which the physician or an immediate family member has a "financial relationship." The Stark Law was passed in response to concerns that these so-called "self-referrals" restrain competition, result in over-utilization of health care services, and ultimately increase health care costs. Since its enactment in 1989, Congress has frequently amended the statute to expand its reach and increase regulation of physician self-referrals.

In addition to the broad ban on self-referrals, the Stark Law prohibits a physician from submitting a claim for services arising from a prohibited referral to the Medicare program or billing any individual, third-party payor, or other entity for these services.

The Stark Law is a "strict liability" statute, meaning that any physician who violates the law, even by accident, may be subject to civil penalties. Penalties for violating the Stark Law can be severe, including denial of payment; required refunds of amounts collected in violation of the law; up to $15,000 in civil monetary penalties for each claim submitted in violation of the law; and up to $100,000 in civil monetary penalties for each arrangement considered to be a circumvention scheme. Further, physicians found in violation can be excluded from participation in federal health care programs, including Medicare.

A whistleblower lawsuit under the False Claims Act can be based on a violation of the Stark Law. For example, if a physician submits claims to Medicare or Medicaid that are the product of prohibited referrals, those claims can form the basis of a whistleblower lawsuit under the False Claims Act. This Act rewards whistleblowers by allowing them to file lawsuits on behalf of the government and share in any money that is recovered from a physician found to have submitted false claims.

Whistleblowers in Stark cases tend to be healthcare administrators, accountants, benefits coordinators, and other healthcare professionals because these individuals are often in the best position to uncover fraudulent referral practices. By blowing the whistle on fraudulent referrals, whistleblowers are often able to collect large amounts of money. Further, the whistleblower laws protect a whistleblower from being fired, demoted, or disciplined for reporting a fraudulent act.

B. GENERAL PROHIBITION ON REFERRALS OF DESIGNATED HEALTH SERVICES

The Stark Law completely prohibits a physician from making referrals for designated health care services payable by Medicare or Medicaid to an entity with which he or she (or an immediate family member) has a financial relationship, unless a specific statutory exception applies. [2]

The Stark Law broadly defines the term "referral." A "referral" means a physician's request for, ordering of, certifying of, or re-certifying of the need for a designated health service. A "referral" also includes the request for a consultation with another physician and any test or procedure ordered by or to be performed by (or under the supervision of) that other physician. Additionally, a "referral" includes the establishment of a plan of care that includes the provision of designated health services.

However, a "referral" does not include designated health services "personally performed or provided" by the referring physician. The Stark Law Regulations state that "a designated health service is not personally performed or provided by the referring physician if it is performed or provided by any other person, including, but not limited to, the referring physician's employees, independent contractors, or group practice members."[3] Thus, the referring physician must directly and personally provide the service to the patient.

For example, if a physician recommends that a patient receive an EKG, the physician would actually have to perform the EKG on the patient in order to avoid this recommendation being classified as a referral under Stark.

A referral can be direct or indirect, meaning that a physician will be considered to have made a referral if they direct another person to make it.[4] Further, referrals may be in any form, including oral, written, or electronic.

---

2 42 U.S.C. § 1395nn(a)(1) (2011).

3 42 C.F. R. 411 351 (2011).

4 42 C.F.R. 411 351

Federal Law 42 U.S.C. Section 1395nn(h)(5) provides the following definition of Referral:

> (A) Physicians' services: Except as provided in subparagraph (C), in the case of an item or service for which payment may be made under part B of this subchapter, the request by a physician for the item or service, including the request by a physician for a consultation with another physician (and any test or procedure ordered by, or to be performed by (or under the supervision of) that other physician), constitutes a "referral" by a "referring physician."
>
> (B) Other items: Except as provided in subparagraph (C), the request or establishment of a plan of care by a physician which includes the provision of the designated health service constitutes a "referral" by a "referring physician."
>
> (C) Clarification respecting certain services integral to a consultation by certain specialists: A request by a pathologist for clinical diagnostic laboratory tests and pathological examination services, a request by a radiologist for diagnostic radiology services, and a request by a radiation oncologist for radiation therapy, if such services are furnished by (or under the supervision of) such pathologist, radiologist, or radiation oncologist pursuant to a consultation requested by another physician does not constitute a "referral" by a "referring physician."

To determine whether a particular referral arrangement will violate the Stark Law, there are three questions that need to be answered. If the answer to each of these questions is "yes," the referral arrangement will violate the Stark Law unless a specific exception applies.

1) Is the patient a Medicare or Medicaid beneficiary?

As previously mentioned, the Stark Law only covers referrals of designated health care services paid for by Medicare or Medicaid, whether in whole or in part. Thus, if the particular patient is not a Medicare or Medicaid beneficiary, then the Stark law would not apply. The Stark Law is not applicable to Medicare HMO (Medicare Advantage Program) patients. It is unclear whether it applies to Medicaid HMO programs, but the safest option is to assume that the Stark Law does apply to these programs and comply with the relevant provisions.

2) Does the entity receiving the referral furnish designated health services?

Federal Law 42 U.S.C. Section 1395nn(h)(6) provides the following definition of Designated Health Services:

(6) The term "designated health services" means any of the following items or services:
(A) Clinical laboratory services.
(B) Physical therapy services.
(C) Occupational therapy services.
(D) Radiology services, including magnetic resonance imaging, computerized axial tomography scans, and ultrasound services.
(E) Radiation therapy services and supplies.
(F) Durable medical equipment and supplies.
(G) Parenteral and enteral nutrients, equipment, and supplies.
(H) Prosthetics, orthotics, and prosthetic devices and supplies.
(I) Home health services.
(J) Outpatient prescription drugs.
(K) Inpatient and outpatient hospital services.
(L) Outpatient speech-language pathology services.

The statute refers to the list of medical billing codes (CPT/HCPCS Codes) to determine which specific services fall under the broad categories described in the above definition of designated health services. Notably, radiology and imaging services include x-rays, ultrasounds, MRIs, nuclear medicine, CT scans, and many other similar services.

Historically, the Stark Law Regulations defined "entity" as the party to which Medicare makes payment for the designated health services; however, this definition was expanded in 2009. The term "entity" now includes both the party that "presented a claim" to Medicare for the designated health service and the party that "performed" the designated health service.

3) Is there a "financial relationship" between the referring physician (or the physician's immediate family member) and the entity receiving the referral?

The term "immediate family member" is defined broadly to include a spouse, child (birth or adopted), sibling, parent, stepparent, stepchild, stepbrother or sister, in-law (father, mother, sister, brother, son, and daughter), grandparent, grandchild, and the spouse of a grandparent or grandchild. A financial relationship involving any of these family members will trigger the Stark Law.

Notably, the definition does not specifically list cousins, aunts, uncles, nieces, and nephews as "immediate family members." Thus, it seems that a financial relationship involving any of these family members would not trigger the Stark Law.

Under the Stark Law, a "financial relationship" exists when the physician or immediate family member has an ownership or investment interest in the entity that furnishes designated health services or if the physician or immediate family member has a compensation arrangement with such an entity.[5]

The Law defines "an ownership or investment interest" as one created "through equity, debt, or other means, and includes an interest in an entity that holds an ownership or investment interest in any entity that furnishes designated health services."[6] A prohibited ownership or investment interest can be direct or indirect.

For example, if a physician refers patients to a physical therapy business in which he owns stock, there is a direct financial relationship. An indirect financial relationship would exist, for example, if a physician refers patients to an MRI Center, and the physician is employed by a group practice that owns shares in the MRI center. Prohibited ownership and investment interests do not include, however, an interest in a retirement plan or ownership of publicly traded securities and mutual funds that meet certain requirements.

Further, the Law broadly defines "compensation arrangement" as "any arrangement involving any remuneration between a physician (or immediate family member of such physician) and an entity," which includes both direct and indirect compensation agreements, whether in cash or in kind.[7] The Regulations specifically state that an "'under arrangements' contract between a hospital and an entity providing designated health services 'under arrangements' to the hospital creates a compensation arrangement for purposes of these regulations."[8] In a typical "under arrangements" agreement, a hospital contracts with a third party to furnish services to the hospital's patients, for which the hospital ultimately bills under its provider number, and the third party receives some sort of compensation to cover the cost of providing the technical services.

The expansive definition of "financial relationship" implicates nearly every financial relationship between physicians and entities that furnish designated health services, thus, physicians must rely on an exception to the Stark law to engage in any type of self-referral.

4) Does an exception apply?

The Stark Law establishes a number of specific exceptions and grants the Secretary of the United States Department of Health and Human Services ("HHS") the authority to create regulatory exceptions for financial relationships that do not pose a risk of program or patient abuse. Each of the Stark Law exceptions has very specific requirements that must be met, which are described in great detail in Sections 411.355–357 of the Stark Law Regulations.[9] Some of the most common Stark Law exceptions are described below.

(A) Office Space. Payments made by a tenant to a landlord for the use of office space will not be considered to be a prohibited compensation arrangement if the following elements are satisfied:[10]

5 42 U.S.C. § 1395nn(a)(2).
6 42 C.F.R. § 411.354 (2011).
7 42 U.S.C. § 1395nn(h)(1).
8 42 C.F.R. § 411.354(5)(c).
9 42 C.F.R. 411.355–411.357.
10 42 C.F.R. 411.357(a).

(i) The lease is set out in writing, signed by the parties, and specifies the premises covered;

(ii) The space leased does not exceed that which is reasonable and necessary for the legitimate business purpose of the lease and is used exclusively by the lessee for legitimate purposes. The lessee may make payments for the use of space consisting of common areas being used at the same time if the payments for common area access do not exceed the pro rata share of expenses for that space based upon the ratio of (a) space used exclusively by the lessee to (b) the total amount of space (other than common areas) occupied by all persons using such common areas, and adjusted to take into account the percentage of full-time usage that occurs in the arrangement;

(iii) The lease provides for a term of rental or lease for at least 1 year, and

(iv) The rental charges over the term of the lease are set in advance, are consistent with fair market value, and are not determined in a manner that takes into account the volume or value of any referrals or other business generated between the parties.

(v) The rental charges over the term of the agreement are not determined using a formula based on:

> 1) a percentage of the revenue raised, earned, bill, collected or otherwise attributable to the services performed or business generated in the office space; or [Note: percentage-based payments are not allowed under this exception].
>
> 2) Per-unit of service rental charges, to the extent that such charges reflect services provided to patients referred by the lessor to the lessee.

There are a number of issues that arise with respect to interpretation of the statute as it applies to medical office leases. These include the following:

> Can the rent vary during the year? The legislative history of the Stark Law indicates that only the method by which payment is to be determined must be fixed in advance. Charges based upon units of time or treatment intervals ("per use" or "per click") may be permitted so long as the rates charged per unit do not fluctuate with the volume or value of referrals between the parties, but the Medicare Anti-Kickback Statute safe harbor regulations do not condone this, so "per use" leases or similar arrangements are not without risk and must be reviewed based on the specific facts and circumstances of the relationship.

Under the federal Anti-Kickback Statute, the aggregate rental charge should be set in advance in order to meet the regulatory safe harbors. The Anti-Kickback safe harbor regulations make it clear that leases that tie rental charges to the use of the rental space on a "per use" or "per procedure" lease will not qualify for protection under the lease safe harbors. Thus, in order to meet the requirements of both the Stark Law and the federal Medicare Anti-Kickback statute, the lease payments should be fixed in advance without variation for use fluctuations, particularly where this would be influenced by the frequency or volume of referrals to the tenant from the landlord.

How is fair market value determined? The Stark Law indicates that fair market value is to be determined without taking into account intended use and without taking into account any additional value attributable to the proximity or convenience to the landlord where the landlord is a potential source of patient referrals. While this causes some confusion as to valuation, it appears that charges need to be based upon overall commercial value of the space used exclusively, such as what a nonmedical user would have to pay to get comparable space.

How is common area usage valued? Payments attributable to the use of common areas, such as utilities and possibly personnel, cannot exceed the tenant's pro rata share of expenses associated with the common areas, which presumably would include maintenance, utilities, and similar expenses. Based upon the common area usage value limitation, the actual value of the use of space where there is a small room and there are valuable common area amenities, may be less than the actual fair market value of the overall rental arrangement.

As an example of the above, assume that four independent physicians each lease an office and examination room in a four-office suit in a hospital's medical office building. Each physician is also entitled to use the suite's common waiting room and reception area. If each office and examination room is exactly the same size, each of the four physicians may pay one-quarter of the rental amount for the common waiting room and reception area.

Can a one year lease qualify even though either party can terminate it without cause prior to the one year term being over? While many advisors believe this is possible, the Center for Medicare and Medicaid Services' (CMS') position is that there needs to be a legally binding one year term, which can only be terminated for "good cause" based upon what normal reasonable grounds for termination of a long term lease would be. Credible authorities believe it is possible to satisfy this requirement by having a one year lease that thereafter continues and permits termination without cause after the initial one year term. The safer approach would be to have the lease continue for subsequent one year terms. If there is a one year lease that thereafter continues and can be terminated by either party without cause, there should be no modification to the terms of the lease unless it then becomes a one year commitment.

(B) Equipment Leases. The exception for equipment leases requires the following:[11]

(i) The lease is set out in writing, is signed by the parties, and specifies the equipment covered by the lease;

(ii) The equipment leased or rented does not exceed what is reasonable and necessary for the legitimate business purposes of the lease and is used exclusively by the lessee when being used by the lessee;

(iii) The lease provides for a term of rental or lease of at least 1 year;

(iv) The rental charges over the term of the lease are set in advance, are consistent with fair market value, and are not determined in a manner that takes into account the volume or value of any referrals or other business generated between the parties;

(v) The rental charges over the term of the agreement are not determined using a formula based on:

1) a percentage of the revenue raised, earned, bill, collected or otherwise attributable to the services performed or business generated in the office space; or [Note: percentage-based payments are not allowed under this exception].

2) Per-unit of service rental charges, to the extent that such charges reflect services provided to patients referred by the lessor to the lessee.

The lease would be commercially reasonable even if no referrals were made between the parties, and

(vii) The lease meets such other requirements as may be imposed by regulations.

11 42 C.F.R. 411.357(b).

The interpretation issues described above for space leases will generally apply for equipment leases as well.

The Stark Law also provides statutory exceptions for employment relationships, personal service arrangements, and physician recruitment. To apply, these statutory exemptions must be strictly followed, and are reprinted below.

(e) Exceptions relating to other compensation arrangements

The following shall not be considered to be a compensation arrangement described in subsection (a)(2)(B) of this section:

...

(2) Bona fide employment relationships. Any amount paid by an employer to a physician (or an immediate family member of such physician) who has a bona fide employment relationship with the employer for the provision of services if—

(A) the employment is for identifiable services,

(B) the amount of the remuneration under the employment—

(i) is consistent with the fair market value of the services, and

(ii) is not determined in a manner that takes into account (directly or indirectly) the volume or value of any referrals by the referring physician,

(C) the remuneration is provided pursuant to an agreement which would be commercially reasonable even if no referrals were made to the employer, and

(D) the employment meets such other requirements as the Secretary may impose by regulation as needed to protect against program or patient abuse.

Subparagraph (B)(ii) shall not prohibit the payment of remuneration in the form of a productivity bonus based on services performed personally by the physician (or an immediate family member of such physician).

(3) Personal service arrangements

(A) In general. Remuneration from an entity under an arrangement (including remuneration for specific physicians' services furnished to a nonprofit blood center) if—

(i) the arrangement is set out in writing, signed by the parties, and specifies the services covered by the arrangement,

(ii) the arrangement covers all of the services to be provided by the physician (or an immediate family member of such physician) to the entity,

(iii) the aggregate services contracted for do not exceed those that are reasonable and necessary for the legitimate business purposes of the arrangement,

(iv) the term of the arrangement is for at least 1 year,

(v) the compensation to be paid over the term of the arrangement is set in advance, does not exceed fair market value, and except in the case of a physician incentive plan described in subparagraph (B), is not determined in a manner that takes into account the volume or value of any referrals or other business generated between the parties,

(vi) the services to be performed under the arrangement do not involve the counseling, promotion, a business arrangement or other activity that violates any State or Federal law, and

(vii) the arrangement meets such other requirements as the Secretary may impose by regulation as needed to protect against program or patient abuse.

...

(5) Physician recruitment. In the case of remuneration which is provided by a hospital to a physician to induce the physician to relocate to the geographic area served by the hospital in order to be a member of the medical staff of the hospital, if—

(A) the physician is not required to refer patients to the hospital,

(B) the amount of the remuneration under the arrangement is not determined in a manner that takes into account (directly or indirectly) the volume or value of any referrals by the referring physician, and

(C) the arrangement meets such other requirements as the Secretary may impose by regulation as needed to protect against program or patient abuse.

Physician Recruitment:

The "physician recruitment" exception described above permits a hospital to remunerate a physician in an effort to induce said physician to relocate his or her practice to the hospital's geographic area and to become a member of the hospital's medical staff, so long as certain requirements are met. However, this exception imposes restrictions on the use of non-competition clauses in the physician's employment contract. The regulations specifically state that "[t]he physician practice may not impose on the recruited physician practice restrictions that unreasonably restrict the recruited physician's ability to practice medicine in the geographic area served by the hospital."[12] This limitation applies when the hospital pays a practice entity-not when the hospital pays the physician directly.

12 42 C.F.R. 411.357(e)(4)(vi).

This regulation is a change from the previous Stark regulations, which completely prohibited the use of non-competition agreements for recruited physicians. In 2007, CMS amended the regulation out of concern that prohibiting physician practices from imposing non-competition agreements would make it more difficult for hospitals to recruit physicians.

In 2011, CMS issued an advisory opinion providing guidance as to the revised regulation regarding the Stark Law restriction on non-competition agreements.[13] This advisory opinion involved a pediatric orthopedic surgeon who was recruited by a hospital to a medical practice. The medical practice wanted to hire the new doctor, but was not willing to do so without a non-competition provision. The non-competition clause restricted "the physician from establishing, operating, or providing professional medical services at any medical office, clinic, or other health care facility at any location within a 25-mile radius of the Hospital for a period of one year following the earlier of the termination of expiration of the Proposed Agreement." CMS concluded that the non-competition agreement did not "unreasonably restrict" the physician's ability to practice medicine in the geographic area because: 1) the time period of one year was reasonable; 2) the distance requirement of 25 miles was reasonable based on the geographic area served by the hospital; 3) the physician could still practice at certain hospitals both within and outside of the hospital's geographic service area without violating the non-competition clause; and 4) the provision complied with the state law.

Therefore, group practices that receive recruitment assistance from hospitals may impose non-competition provisions on recruited physicians, so long as the provisions are reasonable and meet any state law requirements.

C. HOW DOES THE STARK LAW IMPACT A GROUP PRACTICE WHERE PHYSICIANS REFER THEIR OWN PATIENTS FOR GOODS AND SERVICES SOLD BY THE PRACTICE ITSELF?

Many health care practices provide in-office services to which they routinely refer their patients. For example, some practices own, operate, and refer patients to in-office clinical laboratories. Such in-office services are convenient for patients and physicians alike—patients enjoy the convenience of obtaining all medical services in one location while physicians can provide timely and less interrupted services to their patients. However, under the Stark Law, it is impermissible to refer patients for in-office services if the physician has a financial relationship with the providing entity, unless a health care practice qualifies as a "group practice" and complies with several strict requirements.

Qualifying as a "group practice" under the Stark Law enables physicians to take advantage of certain exceptions, including the physician services exception and the in-office ancillary services exception.

1) When is a group of physicians considered to be a "group practice?"

To qualify as a group practice, the group of physicians must meet all of the following requirements, which are further described below:[14]

---

13 Advisory Opinion No. CMS-AO-2011-01 (available at http://www.cms.gov/Medicare/Fraud-and-Abuse/PhysicianSelfReferral/Downloads/CMS-AO-2011-01.pdf).

14 42 U.S.C. § 1395nn(h)(4).

(1) Legal Entity or Entities. The group practice must consist of a single legal entity that uses a single billing number and operates primarily for the purpose of being a medical practice. That legal entity may assume any legal form permitted by the applicable state, e.g., a partnership, professional corporation, limited liability company, and may have 100% wholly owned subsidiaries that offer medical services or products that the group itself can offer.

(2) Two or More Members. The group practice must have at least two physicians who are "members" of the group. The term "member of the group practice" does not include independent contractors. Nor does it include leased employees unless they meet the specific definition of an "employee," which is defined at 42 U.S.C. § 1395nn(h)(2) and indicates that "an individual is considered to be 'employed by' or an 'employee' of an entity if the individual would be considered to be an employee of the entity under the usual common law rules applicable in determining the employer-employee relationship (as applied for purposes of section 3121(d)(2) of the Internal Revenue Code of 1986)."

Note: The Regulations define "member of a group practice" as any one of the following:[15]

(a) A direct or indirect physician owner of a group practice (including a physician whose interest is held by his or her individual professional corporation or by another entity).

(b) A physician employee of the practice group.

(c) A locum tenens physician as defined in 42 C.F.R. 411.351. A Locum tenens physician is defined as "a physician who substitutes (that is, 'stands in the shoes') in exigent circumstances for a physician, in accordance with applicable reassignment rules and regulations."

Note: The term "exigent" means "urgent" or "pressing." Thus, a locum tenens physician is one who works in the place of the regular physician when that physician is absent, when the group practice is short-staffed, or when the practice has some other pressing need for a stand-in physician.

(d) An on-call physician while the physician is providing on-call services for members of the group practice.

(e) A physician is a member of the group during the time that he or she furnishes "patient care services" to the group, as defined in 42 C.F.R. 411.351, which provides that "patient care services" include "any task(s) performed by a physician in the group practice that address the medical needs of specific patients or patients in general, regardless of whether they involve direct patient encounters or generally benefit a particular practice."

15 42 C.F.R. § 411.351.

(3) Full Range of Services. Each physician who is a member of the group must furnish substantially the full range of patient care services through the joint use of shared office space, facilities, equipment, and personnel. This prevents the group from bringing in a specialist and only requiring him or her to perform the most profitable services on the group's patients, while performing other services for patients outside of the group.

(4) Substantially All Services. Substantially all (defined as at least 75% in the aggregate) of the services rendered by the group's member physicians inside and outside of the group must be provided through the group and billed by the group under its billing number, and collections from such billings must be group receipts. This prevents groups from having a large number of part-time physicians who are essentially moonlighting for the group and primarily working in other practices.

(5) Predetermined Formulas. Income and overhead expenses must be distributed in accordance with predetermined formulas, and it is strongly advised that these be set forth in clear written agreements. In other words, the formula for income sharing must be agreed upon before the income is actually earned.

(6) Unified Business. The group must be a "unified business" characterized by centralized decision making and consolidated billing, accounting and financial reporting operations.

(7) Compensation Not Directly or Indirectly Based Upon Volume or Value of Referrals. A group generally may not compensate physicians based directly or indirectly on the volume or value of their referrals, except that a group practice may, in some circumstances, compensate physicians using a productivity bonus or via a profit sharing methodology, as described below.

Federal Law 42 U.S.C. Section 1395nn(h)(4) defines Group Practice as follows:

(4) (A) Definition of group practice

The term "group practice" means a group of 2 or more physicians legally organized as a partnership, professional corporation, foundation, not-for-profit corporation, faculty practice plan, or similar association—

(i) in which each physician who is a member of the group provides substantially the full range of services which the physician routinely provides, including medical care, consultation, diagnosis, or treatment, through the joint use of shared office space, facilities, equipment and personnel,

(ii) for which substantially all of the services of the physicians who are members of the group are provided through the group and are billed under a billing number assigned to the group and amounts so received are treated as receipts of the group,

(iii) in which the overhead expenses of and the income from the practice are distributed in accordance with methods previously determined,

(iv) except as provided in subparagraph (B)(i), in which no physician who is a member of the group directly or indirectly receives compensation based on the volume or value of referrals by the physician,

(v) in which members of the group personally conduct no less than 75 percent of the physician-patient encounters of the group practice.

(vi) which meets such other standards as the Secretary may impose by regulation.

2) What is the physician services exception for group practices?

The Stark Law permits referrals for designated health services that are "physician services" within a group practice, so long as the referred "physician service" is personally performed by or under the personal supervision of a member of, or a physician in, the same group practice as the referring physician.[16] The term "physician services" means professional services performed by physicians, including surgery, consultation, and home, office, and institutional calls.[17]

16 42 U.S.C. § 1395nn(b)(1).

17 42 U.S.C. § 1395x(q); 42 C.F.R. 410.20(a).

While it seems relatively straightforward that another physician in a group practice can "personally perform" certain referred services, the Stark regulations are quite complex when it comes to "incident to" services.

Under the "personal supervision" requirement, physicians may be compensated and given credit for "incident to" services. "Incident to" services are those services performed by other personnel as part of an overall plan of care that is determined and directed by the physician. These services may be billed to Medicare as though the physician personally performed the services.

The Stark Law regulations specifically define "incident to" services as those services and supplies that meet the requirements of the Medicare Benefit Policy Manual.[18]

Thus, in order for the physician to receive credit for "incident to" services, the services must be billed in accordance with Medicare's "incident to" standards. To be covered on an "incident to" basis, the services and supplies must be:

1) An integral (although incidental) part of the physician's professional service. CMS has interpreted this to mean that there must have been a physician's service which initiates the course of treatment during which "incident to" services will be rendered;

2) Commonly rendered without charge or included in the physician's bill; Where supplies are clearly of a type a physician is not expected to have on hand in his/her office or where services are of a type not considered medically appropriate to provide in the office setting, they would not be covered under the "incident to" provision;

3) Of a type that are commonly furnished in physician offices or clinic; and

4) Furnished by the physician or by auxiliary personnel under the physician's direct supervision. There is no requirement that a group practice physician be physically present in the room when the "incident to" services are provided, but the physician must be in the office suite and immediately available to furnish assistance and direction throughout the performance of the procedure.[19] The required supervision can be performed by any physician in the group practice.

18 42 C.F.R. § 411.351

19 42 C.F.R. §410.32(b)(3)(ii).

As an example of the above, an oncologist may be credited for chemotherapy provided "incident to" his or her services, so long as the oncologist directly supervises the administration of the chemotherapy. CMS provides other examples of qualifying "incident to" services, including "cardiac rehabilitation, providing non-self-administrable drugs and other biologicals, and supplies usually furnished by the physician in the course of performing his/her services, e.g., gauze, ointments, bandages, and oxygen."[20]

The CMS Manual provides that "Medicare pays for services and supplies (including drug and biologicals which are not usually self-administered) that are furnished incident to a physician's or other practitioner's services, are commonly included in the physician's or practitioner's bills, and for which payment is not made under a separate benefit category listed in § 1861(s) of the Act. Carriers and intermediaries must not apply incident to requirements to services having their own benefit category. Rather, these services should meet the requirements of their own benefit category. For example, diagnostic tests are covered under §1861(s)(3) of the Act and are subject to their own coverage requirements."[21]

Therefore, only those services that do not have their own separate and independently listed benefit category may be billed as "incident to" a physician service. As noted in the CMS Manual, diagnostic tests have their own category and would not be considered "incident to" services. As a result, clinical laboratory and imaging tests (such as x-rays, MRIs, and PETs) will not qualify and may not be billed as "incident to" services.

Stark therefore strictly prohibits physicians from being paid any portion of monies derived from blood lab billings. While a physician may order a blood law test and read the results of the test, this is considered to be part of the work that the physician is doing for the professional fee he or she receives, and allowing that physician to receive any part of the separate blood lab billing can have serious consequences.

3) What is the in-office ancillary services exception for group practices?

The Stark Law's in-office ancillary services exception generally allows physicians in group practices to provide laboratory, radiology, outpatient prescription drugs, and other designated health services without violating the law.

This exception permits the referral of designated health services, except durable medical equipment (excluding infusion pumps) and parenteral and enteral nutrients, equipment, and supplies, to entities which the physician has a financial relationship, so long as certain requirements are met.[22] Even if the physician organization qualifies as a group practice, three additional requirements must be met before the in-office ancillary services exception is satisfied.

---

20 CMS Medicare Learning Network, Information for Medicare Fee-for-Service Health Care Profesionals, MLN Matters No. SE0441 (available at https://www.cms.gov/Outreach-and-Education/Medicare-Learning-Network-MLN/MLNMattersArticles/downloads/se0441.pdf).

21 Medicare Benefit Policy Manual, Chp. 15, § 60(A), http://www.cms.gov/Regulations-and-Guidance/Guidance/Manuals/Downloads/bp102c15.pdf (last updated June 8, 2012).

22 42 U.S.C. § 1395nn(b)(2).

FURNISHING OF SERVICES BY GROUP MEMBER

The designated health service must be furnished by one of the following: 1) the referring physician; 2) a physician who is in the same group practice as the referring physician 3) an individual who is supervised by the referring physician; or 4) an individual who is supervised by another physician in the same group practice.

LOCATION OF SERVICE REQUIREMENTS

The designated health services must be performed in one of the following:

(a) A "centralized building" used exclusively by the group practice, and not subleased or used by any other practice or business at any time, or

(b) The "same building" where physicians in the group provide the full range of services of patients.[23]

A "centralized building" is a building used by the group practice for: 1) some or all of the group practice's clinical laboratory services; or 2) some or all of its designated health services other than clinical laboratory services. In addition, "centralized building" means that all or part of the building is owned or leased on a full-time basis (i.e., 24 hours per day, 7 days per week for a term of not less than 6 months) by a group practice and is used exclusively by the group practice. A "centralized building" may also include a mobile vehicle, van, or trailer that meets all of these requirements.

Additionally, the designated health service may be performed in the "same building" where physicians in the group provide the full range of services to patients. "Same building" means a structure or combination of structures that share a single street address. Additionally, one of the following requirements must be satisfied in order to meet the "same building" requirement:

1) The referring physician or group practice has an office that is normally open to their patients at least 35 hours per week, and the referring physician or group members regularly practice medicine and furnish physician services, which must include some services that are not designated health services, to patients in that office at least 30 hours per week;

2) The patient usually receives physician services from the referring physician or a member of the group practice, the group practice has an office that is normally open to patients at least 8 hours per week, and the referring physician regularly practices medicine and furnishes physician services, which must include some services that are not designated health services to patients of that office at least 6 hours per week; or

3) The referring physician is present and orders the designated health service during a patient visit on the premises or the referring physician or a member of his or her group practice is present while the designated health service is provided to the patient; the group practice has an office that is normally open to patients at least 8 hours per week, and the referring physician regularly practices medicine and furnishes physician

23 42 C.F.R. § 411.355.

services, which must include some services that are not designated health services, to patients of that office at least 6 hours per week.

BILLING BY GROUP REQUIREMENT

In order to utilize the in-office ancillary services exception, the designated health service must also meet certain billing requirements. The service must be billed by one of the following:

1) The physician performing or supervising the service;

2) The group practice of which the performing/supervising physician is a member under a single billing number assigned to the group practice;

3) An entity that is wholly owned by the performing/supervising physician or such physician's group practice, under the entity's own billing number or under a billing number assigned to the physician or group practice; or

4) An independent third party billing company acting as an agent of the physician, group practice or entity described in the 3 preceding options under a billing number assigned to such physician, group practice or entity.

D. GROUP PRACTICE COMPENSATION

A physician in a Stark Law compliant group practice cannot receive compensation that is directly or indirectly based on the volume or value of the designated health service referrals of the physician, except through certain indirect methods that are deemed to be acceptable under the regulations. These accepted methods of compensation are: 1) overall profit sharing; and 2) productivity bonuses.

Overall profit sharing methods will be acceptable under the Stark Law if the designated health services overall profits are distributed in one of the following ways: [24]

1) Per capita (per member/physician of the group); In this method, the overall profits of all physicians in the group are divided by the number of physicians receiving the profits, and each physician receives an equal share based on this calculation;

2) Based on the distribution of revenues attributed to physician services that are not designated health services; or

3) In any manner, if the revenues of the group derived from designated health services constitute less than 5% of the group's total revenues (including revenues from non-Medicare billings for these services) and the allocated portion of those revenues to each physician in the group practice constitutes 5% or less of his or her total group compensation.

---

24 42 C.F.R. § 411.352.

Additionally, a group practice may pay certain productivity bonuses to its member physicians. A productivity bonus will be acceptable under the Stark Law if any of the following conditions are met:[25]

1) The bonus is based on the physician's total patient encounters or relative value units produced, including each physician's "incident to" services;

2) The bonus is based on the allocation of the physician's compensation that is not related to designated health services; or

3) Designated health services revenues of the group practice are less than 5% of total revenues, and the allocated portion of those revenues to each physician in the group constitutes 5% or less of his or her total group compensation.

A group practice is not required to use the same profit sharing methodology for all of the physicians within the group. The Stark Law regulations permit group practices to adopt a "cost center" approach to physician compensation, allowing each center to make decisions about compensating physicians within the center. Under the regulations, profits for designated health services may be "pooled" and segregated within subsets, so long as each subset has at least five physicians and meets the Stark Law requirements described above.[26] After the profits from designated health services are divided, the physicians within each subset can be paid a share of the overall profits accruing to that particular subset. Although the Stark Law regulations do not impose strict limitations on how these subsets can be organized, the regulations do not allow physicians to be "directly or indirectly" compensated based on the volume or value of their referrals. Therefore, these subsets should not be established based on the number or value of referrals made to these physicians by the group.

The following sample language can be used to facilitate compliance with these rules:

CASH FLOW AND EXPENSE ALLOCATIONS

Each Member will be calculated and paid on a quarterly basis, based upon calculations made for each calendar quarter which shall be based upon the applicable Member's Revenue Allocation, less such Member's Expense Allocation, as described below.

The Member's Revenue Allocations shall be based upon receipts attributable to professional services rendered by such Member and a proportion of all receipts of the medical practice that do not constitute compensation for professional services rendered by a Member. Revenue shall therefore include receipts from services rendered by non-member employed physicians and practice extenders, receipts attributable to the billings for x-ray, bone density scan, and other non-professional technical components services, and receipts attributable to medical directorship fees, which shall be allocated pro rata to professional service fees of the applicable Members. For example, if one Member's receipts constitute 26% of the receipts attributable to professional services rendered by all Members, then 26% of ancillary service receipts and receipts from employed non-member physicians and practice extenders shall be credited to such member.

---

25 42 C.F.R. § 411.352.

26 42 C.F.R. 411.352(i)(2).

The Member's Expense Allocation, which will determine the amounts to be subtracted from the Member's Revenue Allocation to determine revenue distributions, shall be based upon the following four categories of expenses:

1. Fixed Expenses ("50/50 Items") multiplied by a fraction, the numerator of which will be one (1), and the denominator of which shall be the total number of Members (50% initially);

2. Variable Expenses shall be allocated pro rata to the allocation of professional service compensation described in Section _____ revenues under Section ____ of this Agreement. For example, a Member allocated 58% of revenues under Section ______ will be charged with 58% of the Variable Expenses.

3. Direct Expenses. Each Member agrees to pay any and all Direct Expenses directly by such Member so that such expenses are not expenditures of the Company, but any such expenditure by the Company that would be a Direct Expense of a Member or its Named Physician shall constitute a Direct Expense for purposes of this Agreement and as set forth below.

4. Direct Expenses. Each Member agrees to pay any and all Direct Expenses directly by such Member so that such expenses are not expenditures of the Company, but any such expenditure by the Company that would be a Direct Expense of a Member or its Named Physician shall constitute a Direct Expense for purposes of this Agreement and as set forth below.

   In order to facilitate cash flow and distributions to the Members during the course of each calendar month the Manager may estimate their respective shares of the excess of their Revenue Allocation over their allocated General Expenses, Variable Expenses, and Direct Expenses, and may receive distributions of mutually agreeable amounts periodically during the month, provided that an accounting shall be performed by the fifteenth (15th) day of the second calendar month after the end of each calendar month and each Member shall reimburse, or shall be reimbursed, for the difference between their actual share and that received by the Member during the applicable calendar month, as and when subsequently calculated by the certified public accountant for the Company. The Members recognize that expenses and obligations of the Company must be paid and kept current, and that payments of distributions to the Members shall be reduced to the extent necessary so that there is sufficient cash flow such that third party creditors and suppliers are paid in the normal course of business.

   General Expenses ("50/50 Items") are those expenses considered to primarily occur notwithstanding the relative and respective volume of production or facility use by the Key Professional Employees, and may include the following:

   1.A. All expenses pertaining to lease payments and obligations under all lease agreements for use of the practice office and amenities therein;

   1.B. Expenses relating to the Company's furniture, equipment, computer systems, and any and all equipment leasing and maintenance costs with reference to the physical assets of the Company;

1.C. Accounting fees, except for those fees for services specific to, and which solely benefit, only one Member;

1.D. Water, sewer, garbage service and common storage;

1.E. Casualty, fire, theft and other insurances with respect to maintaining the office, including all insurances required by the lease agreement;

1.F. Any and all liability and malpractice insurance coverage for the Company itself;

1.G. Legal fees, except those fees for services specific to, and which solely benefit, only one Member;

1.H. Magazines for the waiting room as mutually agreed between the parties;

1.I. Utilities;

1.J. Janitorial services;

1.K. Other expenses not described below that are properly categorized as items that occur regardless of patient activity, including maintenance and repair of all items used in the Practice, service contracts for equipment, locksmiths, pest control, and any maintenance required under applicable Leases or otherwise in the Practice.

Variable Expenses are those expenses considered to vary based upon the volume of use and production in the practice, and thus more equitably suited to be divided pro rata to productivity as opposed to equally, as determined by the Manager or Managers on a reasonable basis, and to initially include the following:

2.A. Any and all drugs, medical, and business supplies ordered for the Practice;

2.B. General office expenses and supplies including stationary, typing (other than medical transcription), paper products, postage, x-ray film, x-ray chemicals, computer paper, printer cartridges, subscriptions and health books for patients;

2.C. Salaries and compensation, worker's compensation, and other expenses, including taxes, benefits and pension contributions of all business office and nursing personnel, except for the business manager, and physician assistant compensation, taxes and benefits with respect to physician assistants assist a particular named Key Professional Employee of a Member;

Salaries for the administrative personnel (which are intended initially to include only an office manager and front desk personnel), but excluding the spouses of the Named Physicians and billing personnel;

2.D. Expenses of general employee courses, gifts, educational seminars, office parties, luncheons, and other employee events provided by the Practice including on premises and off premises employee events;

2.E. Pension plan contributions attributable to all employees other than the Key Professional Employees, business manager and physician assistants and/or surgical assistants with respect to physician assistants and/or surgical assistants who assist a particular named Key Professional Employee of a Member, and accrued to the extent deemed appropriate by the Certified Public Accountant for the Company if and when there is a transition of ownership in the Company so that each Member is responsible for their fair share thereof; and

2.F. Any and all advertising, including Yellow Page listings and brochures, but only to the extent approved by all Members;

2.G. Promotional expenses agreed to by all Members;

2.H. Business Telephone Expenses;

Direct Expenses are those expenses that are not treated as General Expenses ("50/50 Items") or Variable Expenses and will be the responsibility of the Member incurring them, but if paid by the Company such payment shall be deducted or credited from the distribution otherwise payable to the particular member that has benefitted, or will be repaid immediately upon request of the other Member. Such Direct Expenses shall include the following:

3.A. Automobile expenses;

3.B. Promotion and other expenses with respect to publishing activities of any Member;

3.C. Books, educational expenses, educational trips, society memberships, or other individual professional expenses;

3.D. Amounts paid for the purchase or lease of a car or mobile phones, or PDAs, or the monthly charges and service fees relating thereto;

3.E. Health, workers' compensation and disability insurance for each Key Professional Employee and their families;

3.F. Expenses with respect to any physician assistant, surgical assistant, physician extender, employee or contractor who works solely for or at the request of one Member including salaries, health insurance, workers' compensation insurance, retirement plan benefits, educational seminars, and malpractice insurance for physicians assistants;

3.G. Expenses for medical transcription services for each Member;

3.H. Malpractice insurance as to each Member, and the cost of malpractice insurance to the Company to the extent equitably allocated to such Member based upon the relative cost of malpractice insurance for each Member covering the Company;

3.I. Occupational licenses for each Member;

3.J. Any and all payroll taxes and pension plan contributions attributable to each Member or such Member's primary physician and any spouse and child thereof, as well as compensation paid to such individuals; and

3.K. Any Yellow Page listings or advertising expenses ordered by a Member and not approved by all Members.

Further, any and all compensation paid to a Key Professional Employee by the respective Members shall be the sole responsibility of such Member. Expenses described above for a "Member" shall include any expenses allocable to or for the benefit of the Key Professional Employee of such Member.

Any expense not clearly categorized as a Fixed Expense, Variable Expense, or Direct Expense, shall be characterized in a fair and reasonable manner, consistent with the guidelines set forth above and the intentions of the parties in establishing such guidelines.

The calculations described above may be made for any short period that may apply during the term of any month to facilitate calculation if any Member terminates from the Company during a month, or the results for such month may be pro rated if determined appropriate by a majority of the Members. No Member shall be obligated to pay for any General Expenses attributable to any time period from and after such Member's withdrawal from the Company or the termination of Employment of such Member's Key Professional Employee, except as otherwise provided.

The above allocations and formulas may be modified by a written attachment or other summary agreed to between the parties, or at minimum by ___% of the Members, provided that any such modification must be entered into in advance of the period of time for which it applies with notice to all Members.

E. REPORTING REQUIREMENTS

1. Voluntary Self-Disclosure of Law Breaches - Tag CMS Before CMS Tags You!

The Patient Protection and Affordable Care Act provides for the establishment of a voluntary self-disclosure protocol, under which providers can self-disclose actual or potential violations of the Stark Law. Pursuant to this Act, the Centers for Medicare and Medicaid Services (CMS) created a self-disclosure protocol to facilitate the resolution of matters that are actual or potential violations of the Stark Law.[27]

CMS published a manual providing specific instructions for self-disclosures, which can be found on the CMS website.[28]

Any health care provider or supplier, whether an individual or an entity, may make disclosures through the self-disclosure process, if the provider or supplier believes that its conduct amounts to an actual or potential violation of the Stark Law. However, the manual cautions that that this process should not to be used to check compliance with the Stark Law and explicitly states CMS has a separate advisory opinion process for such inquiries. The CMS manual provides that "a disclosing party should make a submission to the SRDP with the intention of resolving its overpayment liability exposure for the conduct it identified."[29]

---

27 Whether, when, to where and how to disclose a Stark law violation is a difficult and complex decision that should not be made without competent legal counsel.

28 CMS Voluntary Disclosure Protocol, https://www.cms.gov/Medicare/Fraud-andAbuse/

29 Id.

Additionally, this self-disclosure process is not available for violations of both the Stark Law and the federal Anti-Kickback Statute. Conduct that raises liability risks under both the Stark Law and the Anti-Kickback Statute should be disclosed through the Office of Inspector General's self-disclosure protocol rather than through the CMS voluntary-self disclosure protocol. If CMS determines that the disclosed information could potentially be a violation of the Anti-Kickback Statute or other non-Stark laws, it may make referrals to the OIG and/or the Department of Justice. Thus, before submitting a disclosure it is important to consider the appropriate place to disclose an actual or potential violation. The CMS manual provides the specific process for disclosure as follows:

> The disclosure must be submitted electronically to 1877SRDP@cms.hhs.gov. In addition, the disclosing party must submit an original and 1 copy by mail to the Division of Technical Payment Policy, ATTN: Provider and Supplier Self-Disclosure, Centers for Medicare and Medicaid Services, 7500 Security Boulevard, Mailstop C4-25-02, Baltimore, MD 21244-1850. Submissions by facsimile will not be accepted. When the disclosing party submits a disclosure electronically, CMS will immediately send a response email acknowledging receipt of the submission. After reviewing the submission, CMS will send a letter to the disclosing party or its representative either accepting or rejecting the disclosure.[30]

Proper disclosure should be made in a timely fashion after discovering the potential or actual violation. The manual establishes a deadline for reporting and returning overpayments, which is the later of: (1) the date which is 60 days after the date on which the overpayment was identified; or (2) the date any corresponding cost report is due, if applicable.

The CMS manual also provides an extensive list of requirements that must be included in a proper disclosure:

1) The name, address, provider and tax I.D. number of the disclosing party; and the names and addresses of any related entities, and any affected corporate divisions, departments or branches; and the name and address of the disclosing party's designated representative;

2) A description of the nature of the matter being disclosed, including the type of financial relationship, the parties involved, the time periods during which the violation occurred, the date the violation stopped, the type of designated health service claims at issue, the type of transaction or conduct giving rise to the self disclosure, the names of the entities and individuals believed to be implicated, and an explanation of their roles in the matter;

3) A statement by the disclosing party explaining why it believes a Stark Law violation may have occurred, including a complete legal analysis of the Stark Law's applicability to the conduct, an explanation as to whether any Stark Law exceptions were met or not met, and a description of the potential causes of the problem;

4) How the disclosed matter was discovered and the steps taken to address the problem;

30 Id.

5) A statement identifying whether the disclosing party has a history of similar conduct, or has any prior criminal, civil, and regulatory enforcement actions (including payment suspensions) against it;

6) A description of the existence and adequacy of a pre-existing compliance program that the disclosing party had, and all efforts by the disclosing party to prevent a recurrence of the incident or practice in the affected division as well as in any related health care entities. A description of the measures or actions taken by the disclosing party to restructure the arrangement or non-compliant relationship;

7) A description of appropriate notices, if applicable, provided to other Government agencies;

8) Whether the disclosing party has knowledge that the matter is under current inquiry by a Government agency or contractor. If the disclosing party has knowledge of a pending inquiry, identify any such Government agency or contractor, and the individual representatives involved, if known.

9) Whether it is under investigation or other inquiry for other matters relating to a Federal health care program, including any matters it has disclosed to other Government entities, and provide similar information relating to those other matters.

A disclosing party must also submit a financial analysis relating to any actual or potential violations and submit the findings with its initial disclosure. The financial analysis must:

1) Set forth the total amount, itemized by year, that is actually or potentially due and owing based upon the applicable "look back" period. The "look back" period is the time during which the disclosing party may not have been in compliance with the physician self-referral law.

2) Describe the methodology used to set forth the amount that is actually or potentially due and owing. Indicate whether estimates were used, and, if so, how they were calculated.

3) Set forth the total amount of remuneration a physician(s) received as a result of an actual or potential violation(s) based upon the applicable "look back" period.

4) Provide a summary of any auditing activity undertaken and a summary of the documents the disclosing party has relied upon relating to the actual or potential violation(s) disclosed.

Lastly, the disclosing party must include a signed certificate "stating that, to the best of the individual's knowledge, the information provided contains truthful information and is based on a good faith effort to bring the matter to CMS' attention for the purpose of resolving the disclosed potential liabilities relating to the physician self-referral law."[31]

---

31 Id.

Once CMS receives the disclosure, it will begin its verification process. To facilitate its inquiry, CMS may request additional information, such as financial statements, income tax returns, and other documents, if needed. If additional information is requested, a disclosing party will be given at least 30 days to furnish the information. The disclosing party is expected to cooperate with CMS in good faith and provide all requested documents.

After CMS completes its inquiry, it will determine the amounts owed. CMS may reduce the amounts owed based on a consideration of the following factors: (1) the nature and extent of the improper or illegal practice; (2) the timeliness of the self-disclosure; (3) the cooperation in providing additional information related to the disclosure; (4) the litigation risk associated with the matter disclosed; and (5) the financial position of the disclosing party.[32] Although CMS may reduce the amount owed, it is under no obligation to do so. CMS will not accept any payments until the inquiry is completed, but it is recommended to put available funds in an interest-bearing escrow account to ensure that these funds will be accessible if needed. While CMS is investigating the inquiry, the disclosing party may not make any payments relating to the matter in question to any Federal health care program without prior consent from CMS.

2. Stark Law's Disclosure Upon Request Rules

The Stark Law provides that every entity that furnishes designated health services must provide the Department of Health and Human Services with "information concerning the entity's ownership, investment, and compensation arrangements"[33] upon request. This statute only requires that information be submitted upon request by the Department of Health and Human Services and does not require the entity to submit annual reports. However, the following items must be submitted upon request:

1) The covered items and services provided by the entity;

2) The names and identification numbers of all physicians with an ownership or investment interest, or with a compensation arrangement, in the entity, or whose immediate family members have an ownership or investment interest or compensation arrangement with the entity;

The statute provides that this requirement does not apply to designated health services provided outside of United States or to entities which are determined by the Secretary to provide services for which Medicare pays for very infrequently.

Failing to meet the reporting requirements can result in severe penalties. Any person who fails to make a required reporting is subject to a civil monetary penalty of $10,000 for each day that the information is not reported.

---

32 Id.

33 42 U.S.C. 1395nn(f).

CHAPTER 3
THE FEDERAL ANTI-KICKBACK STATUTE

A. SUMMARY OF THE FEDERAL ANTI-KICKBACK STATUTE

The federal Anti-Kickback Statute strictly prohibits the offer, solicitation, payment, or receipt of any remuneration, in cash or in kind, in return for, or to induce, the referral of a patient for any service that may be paid by a Federal Health Care Program (most notably, Medicare, Medicare HMO, Medicaid, Medicaid HMO services, TriCare and Federal Employee Health Benefit Plans).[34] Prohibited conduct also includes remuneration in return for purchasing, leasing, ordering, or arranging for (or recommending the purchase, lease, or order of) any good, facility, service, or item reimbursed under Medicare or a state health care program.

Remuneration has been broadly defined to encompass anything of value. The OIG opined in Advisory Opinion in 2008 that any "opportunity to generate fees" can constitute remuneration.[35] One court even ruled that an "opportunity to bill" for patient services constituted remuneration in the context of allowing doctors first priority to unassigned patients in a hospital setting.[36]

Although the Anti-Kickback Statute imposes a "knowing and willful" intent requirement, the Patient Protection and Affordable Care Act of 2010[37] clarified the ambiguity of this intent requirement by adding a provision which states that actual knowledge of an Anti-Kickback Statute violation or the specific intent to commit a violation of the Anti-Kickback Statute is not necessary for conviction under the statute.

The core of a violation of the Anti-Kickback Statute is "inducement," not necessarily the structure of the arrangement.[38] Consequently, the relevant inquiry in each case focuses on the subjective intent of the parties to exchange remuneration for referrals.[39] Intent need not be expressed, but may be inferred. For example, one court found that where the purchase price of a private medical practice or payment for services rendered under a compensation arrangement exceeded fair market value, the amount paid in excess of fair market value was "intended" as payment for the referral of program-related business.[40]

---

34 42 U.S.C. § 1320a-7(b).

35 Advisory Opinion 08-10, August 26, 2008.

36 See United States ex rel. Fry v. The Health Alliance of Greater Cincinnati, et al. (Christ Hospital of Cincinnati), No. C-1-03-167 (S.D. Ohio Feb. 2, 2010). In this case, an AKS violation was based on the hospital providing priority access to unassigned heart station patients to community cardiologists based directly on the volume of their referrals to the hospital.

37 Patient Protection and Affordable Care Act of 2010, Pub. L. No. 111-148, PPACA § 6402(f)(2), amending 42 U.S.C. § 1320a-7b.

38 United States v. Bay State Ambulance & Hosp. Rental Serv., 874 F.2d 20, 30 (1st Cir. 1989).

39 Preamble to 42 C.F.R. Part § 1001, 56 Fed. Reg. 35952, 35955 (7/29/91).

40 United States v. Lipkis, 770 F.2d 1447 (9th Cir. 1985)

B. SANCTIONS FOR VIOLATING THE FEDERAL ANTI-KICKBACK STATUTE

The federal Anti-Kickback Statute provides criminal penalties for individuals or entities who knowingly and willfully solicit or receive any remuneration (including any kickback, bribe, or rebate) directly or indirectly, in cash or kind, in return for referring an individual for any item or medical service reimbursed under any federal health care program.

Under the statue, violations are classified as a felony, which imposes a fine of up to $25,000 and a term of imprisonment for up to five years. A violation of the federal Anti-Kickback Statute can also give rise to federal health care program exclusion, civil monetary penalties of up to $50,000 per offense, and liability under the False Claims Act. In an Anti-Kickback case, the OIG may seek a penalty of up to $50,000 for each improper act and damages of up to three times the amount of remuneration at issue! Therefore, violators of this statute could potentially face huge fines, jail time, and exclusion from federal health care programs.

If a physician is excluded from participating in federal health care programs due to a violation of the federal Anti-Kickback statute or other law discussed in this book,[41] then Medicare, Medicaid, TRICARE, and the Veterans Health Administration, among others, will not pay for items or services that the physician provides or prescribes. The physician cannot directly bill for treating Medicare patients, and he or she cannot bill indirectly through a group practice. This also extends to payment for administrative and management services not directly related to patient care. Additionally, monies received from a federal program cannot be used to pay an excluded physician's salary, expenses, or fringe benefits. Excluded physicians, can, however, continue to render medical services to non-federal or state healthcare beneficiaries.

The Balanced Budget Act of 1997 allows civil monetary penalties to be imposed against entities that employ excluded physicians or individuals to provide services to Medicare beneficiaries.[42] A group practice that submits claims to Medicare or any other federal health care program for services provided by excluded physicians can face significant liability. Physicians and practices can face penalties of up to $10,000 for each item or service furnished that is listed on a claim for a federal program reimbursement. Additionally, there can be an assessment of up to three times the amount claimed. The practice itself could also face exclusion if it tries to claim a reimbursement for items or services rendered by the excluded physician.[43]

In order to avoid potential liability, it is crucial for health care providers and entities to check the OIG List of Excluded Individuals/Entities on the OIG website (www.hhs.gov/oig) prior to hiring or contracting with individuals or entities. In addition, if they have not already done so, health care providers should periodically check the OIG website for determining the participation/exclusion status of current employees and contractors. The website contains OIG program exclusion information and is updated in both on-line searchable and downloadable formats, which is updated on a monthly basis.

---

41 42 U.S.C.A. § 1320a-7.

42 42 C.F.R. § 1003.102.

43 Special Advisory Bulletin: The Effect of Exclusion from Participation in Federal Health Care Programs, Office of Inspector General, available at http://oig.hhs.gov/fraud/docs/alertsandbulletins/effected.htm (September 1999).

C. "ONE PURPOSE" REQUIREMENT

United States v. Greber[44] is the leading case applying the "one purpose" requirement. In this case, Dr. Greber was paid by a diagnostic testing service provider for readings of his patients' holter monitor tests. Dr. Greber admitted that one purpose of the arrangement was so that he could be compensated for referrals. The Third Circuit upheld Dr. Greber's conviction by interpreting the Anti-Kickback Statute broadly and holding that liability attaches so long as any one of the subjective purposes of the remuneration is to induce referrals, even if there are other legitimate purposes to the arrangement.[45] Greber also is noteworthy for equating payments for professional services in excess of the Medicare professional component (and thereby fair market value) with a quid pro quo for patient referrals.

D. "SAFE HARBORS"

The Medicare and Medicaid Patient and Program Protection Act of 1987 required the United States Department of Health and Human Services to promulgate regulations specifying and protecting payment practices encompassing legitimate business practices (so-called "safe harbors") that will not be subject to criminal prosecution or exclusion from the Medicare and Medicaid as involving prohibited remuneration.

While the safe harbor regulations protect certain specified arrangements from prosecution under the Anti-Kickback Statute,[46] an arrangement must meet all of the elements of a safe harbor to be explicitly permitted. A payment practice is not necessarily illegal because it fails to comply with a safe harbor, but the statute is written very broadly, and it is best to always fit within a safe harbor or to get advice from a well versed health care lawyer before proceeding with conduct that is not specifically safe harbored.

When a payment practice serves "multiple purposes," it will only be protected if it falls into a safe harbor for each purpose. For example, if a payment is made to compensate for personal services and equipment rental, the payment practice will be protected only if it fits into both the personal service and equipment rental safe harbors. Thus, compliance with only one safe harbor will not insulate payment practices serving multiple functions, if another purpose of the payment practice is implemented in a manner that violates the statute.[47]

1) Investment Interests Safe Harbors[48]

Investment Interests in $50,000,000 Plus Companies.

Any payment made as a return on an investment to an investor, such as a dividend or interest, will be protected under very narrow circumstances. First, the safe harbor protects investments in large publicly traded corporations listed on a registered national securities exchange

---

44 760 F.2d 68 (3d Cir. 1985), cert. denied, 474 U.S. 988 (1985).

45 Id. at 69.

46 P.L. No. 100-93, 100 Stat. 688 (1987)

47 Id. at 35957.

48 42 C.F.R. § 1001.952(a).

that own more than $50 million in non-depreciated net tangible assets.[49] The OIG clarified in its 1999 regulations that only assets or revenues related to the furnishing of healthcare items or services will be counted for purposes of qualifying for the $50 million asset threshold.

Small Investment Interests Where No More than 40% Ownership is Held by Referring Individuals and/or Entities

This safe harbor encompasses limited and general partnership interests, shareholders, and holders of debt securities where either of two standards is met.[50] The two standards set forth in the small entities safe harbor are known as the "60-40" rules.

Under the first 60-40 rule (the "60-40 investor rule"), no more than 40% of the value of the investment interest in each class of investment may be held in the previous fiscal year or 12-month period by investors who were in a position to make or influence referrals, furnish items or services to, or otherwise general business for the entity.[51]

Under the second rule (the "60-40 revenue rule"), no more than 40% of the gross revenue of the entity in the previous fiscal year or previous 12-month period may come from referrals, items or services furnished, or business otherwise generated from investors.[52] The OIG clarified in its 1999 regulations that only assets or revenues related to the furnishing of healthcare items or services will be counted for purposes of qualifying for the 60/40 gross revenue test.

Other requirements of the Investment Interests Safe Harbor include:

(i) The investment terms for an investor who is in a position to influence referrals must be no different than those offered to a passive investor.

(ii) The investment terms must not be related to the expected value or volume of referrals.

(iii) The investment terms may not require that a passive investor make referrals to the entity.

(iv) All marketing of the entity's items or services must be on the same terms to passive investors as to non-investors.

(v) Neither the entity nor any investor may loan funds to an investor or guarantee a loan for an investor who is in a position to influence referrals or otherwise generate business for the entity, for the purpose of using any part of the loan

49 42 C.F.R. § 1001.952(a)(1). The July 21, 1994, proposed regulations would require that the minimum $50 million in assets be "related to the furnishing of health care."

50 42 C.F.R. § 1001.952(a)(1). The July 21, 1994, proposed regulations would require that the minimum $50 million in assets be "related to the furnishing of health care."

51 42 C.F.R. § 1001-952(a)(2)(1).

52 42 C.F.R. § 1001.952(a)(2)(vi). The July 21, 1994, proposed regulations would clarify that the 40% test is applied to gross revenue "related to the furnishing of health care items," and not to all gross revenue.

proceeds to purchase an investment interest in the entity.

(vi) The return on the investor's return for the investment interest must be proportionate to the amount of capital contributed by the investor.

2) Ownership Interests in Compliant Solo or Group Practices

Physicians are protected when they invest in their own solo or group practices, as long as the practice meets the specified requirements. The equity interests in the practice or group must be held by licensed professionals who practice as part of the group and those interests must be in the practice or group itself rather than in a subdivision. In addition, the group practice must be organized as a "unified business with centralized decision-making, pooling of expenses and revenues, and a comprehensive/profit distribution system that is not based on satellite offices operating substantially as if they were separate enterprises or profit centers." The group practice must also meet the Stark Law definition of a "group practice" (set forth in 42 C.F.R. § 411.352 and discussed in Chapter II above), and the revenues from ancillary services must be derived from "in-office ancillary services" that meet the Stark Law requirements.[53]

3) Space, Equipment, and Personal Service Arrangements

There are three separate safe harbors for space rentals, equipment leases, and personal service and management contracts,[54] but the requirements of these three safe harbors are substantially the same. To qualify for these safe harbors, the following four requirements must be met:

(i) The agreement must be in writing, setting out all the relevant terms, and has to signed by all parties;

(ii) Is for a term of not less than one year;

(iii) The aggregate services or space contracted for do not exceed those that are reasonably necessary to accomplish the commercially reasonable business purpose of the personal services or rental; and

(iv) The charge reflects fair market value.

If any of the above requirements are not met, then the arrangement is probably not safe under the Anti-Kickback Statute.

To fully comply with this safe harbor, the agreement must be for a term of "at least one year," but an agreement terminable before one year may be acceptable if the other requirements of the safe harbor are met, particularly where termination is for cause. However, if the contract is cancelled before the anniversary date, the parties may not enter into a similar arrangement under different terms before the anniversary date of the original contract.

53 42 C.F.R. § 1001.952(p). There are additional requirements for group practices.

54 42 C.F.R. § 1001.952(b),(c),(d)

It is extremely important to recognize that the rent payable may be extremely small in an office sharing lease agreement in which the space is occupied by the tenant less than the full amount of time that the office is open. An OIG report on space leases specifically states that "[t]he supplier's rent should be calculated based on the ratio of the time the space is in use by the supplier to the total amount of time the physician's office is in use. In addition, the rent should be calculated based on the ratio of the amount of space that is used exclusively by the supplier to the total amount of space in the physician's office."[55] Thus, if the space is not leased for a significant amount of time, the amount of rent may not be very high.

42 C.F.R. 1001.952(b), (c), and (d) provide:

> (b) Space rental. As used in section 1128B of the Act, "remuneration" does not include any payment made by a lessee to a lessor for the use of premises, as long as all of the following six standards are met—
>
> > (1) The lease agreement is set out in writing and signed by the parties.
> >
> > (2) The lease covers all of the premises leased between the parties for the term of the lease and specifies the premises covered by the lease.
> >
> > (3) If the lease is intended to provide the lessee with access to the premises for periodic intervals of time, rather than on a full-time basis for the term of the lease, the lease specifies exactly the schedule of such intervals, their precise length, and the exact rent for such intervals.
> >
> > (4) The term of the lease is for not less than one year.
> >
> > (5) The aggregate rental charge is set in advance, is consistent with fair market value in arms-length transactions and is not determined in a manner that takes into account the volume or value of any referrals or business otherwise generated between the parties for which payment may be made in whole or in part under Medicare, Medicaid or other Federal health care programs.
> >
> > (6) The aggregate space rented does not exceed that which is reasonably necessary to accomplish the commercially reasonable business purpose of the rental.
> > Note that for purposes of paragraph (b) of this section, the term fair market value means the value of the rental property for general commercial purposes, but shall not be adjusted to reflect the additional value that one party (either the prospective lessee or lessor) would attribute to the property as a result of its proximity or convenience to sources of referrals or business otherwise generated for which payment may be made in whole or in part under Medicare, Medicaid and all other Federal health care programs.
>
> (c) Equipment rental. As used in section 1128B of the Act, "remuneration" does not include any payment made by a lessee of equipment to the lessor of the equipment for the use of the equipment, as long as all of the following six standards are met—

55 OIG Special Fraud Alert: Rental of Space in Physicians Offices by Persons or Entities to Which Physicians Refer (Feb. 2000) (available at http://oig.hhs.gov/fraud/docs/alertsandbulletins/office%20space.htm).

(1) The lease agreement is set out in writing and signed by the parties.

(2) The lease covers all of the equipment leased between the parties for the term of the lease and specifies the equipment covered by the lease.

(3) If the lease is intended to provide the lessee with use of the equipment for periodic intervals of time, rather than on a full-time basis for the term of the lease, the lease specifies exactly the schedule of such intervals, their precise length, and the exact rent for such interval.

(4) The term of the lease is for not less than one year.

(5) The aggregate rental charge is set in advance, is consistent with fair market value in arms-length transactions and is not determined in a manner that takes into account the volume or value of any referrals or business otherwise generated between the parties for which payment may be made in whole or in part under Medicare, Medicaid or all other Federal health care programs.

(6) The aggregate equipment rental does not exceed that which is reasonably necessary to accomplish the commercially reasonable business purpose of the rental. Note that for purposes of paragraph (c) of this section, the term fair market value means that the value of the equipment when obtained from a manufacturer or professional distributor, but shall not be adjusted to reflect the additional value one party (either the prospective lessee or lessor) would attribute to the equipment as a result of its proximity or convenience to sources of referrals or business otherwise generated for which payment may be made in whole or in part under Medicare, Medicaid or other Federal health care programs.

(d) Personal services and management contracts. As used in section 1128B of the Act, "remuneration" does not include any payment made by a principal to an agent as compensation for the services of the agent, as long as all of the following seven standards are met—

(1) The agency agreement is set out in writing and signed by the parties.

(2) The agency agreement covers all of the services the agent provides to the principal for the term of the agreement and specifies the services to be provided by the agent.

(3) If the agency agreement is intended to provide for the services of the agent on a periodic, sporadic or part-time basis, rather than on a full-time basis for the term of the agreement, the agreement specifies exactly the schedule of such intervals, their precise length, and the exact charge for such intervals.

(4) The term of the agreement is for not less than one year.

(5) The aggregate compensation paid to the agent over the term of the agreement is set in advance, is consistent with fair market value in arms-length transactions and is not determined in a manner that takes into account the volume or value of any referrals or business otherwise generated between the parties for which payment may be made in whole or in part under Medicare, Medicaid or other Federal health care programs.

(6) The services performed under the agreement do not involve the counselling or promotion of a business arrangement or other activity that violates any State or Federal law.

(7) The aggregate services contracted for do not exceed those which are reasonably necessary to accomplish the commercially reasonable business purpose of the services.

For purposes of paragraph (d) of this section, an agent of a principal is any person, other than a bona fide employee of the principal, who has an agreement to perform services for, or on behalf of, the principal.

4) Sale of Practice

This safe harbor permits the sale of a practice by one practitioner to another practitioner and is extremely narrow. It requires that the selling practitioner not be in a position to make referrals or otherwise generate business for the purchasing practitioner after one year from the date of sale.56 As a practical matter, this safe harbor is only available if the selling practitioner is retiring from the practice or leaving the service area.

In 1999, the OIG expanded the safe harbor protection to include the sale of a practice by a practitioner to a hospital in an underserved area.57 For payments made to a practitioner by a hospital to qualify under the safe harbor and not be treated as remuneration: (1) the sale must be completed within three years; (2) the selling practitioner must not be in a position to make referrals to or generate business for the purchasing hospital or entity after the sale; (3) the practice must be located in a Health Professional Shortage Area ("HPSA") for the practitioner's particular specialty; and (4) the hospital or other purchasing entity must, in good faith, engage in recruitment activities to find a new practitioner to take over the acquired practice.

5) Employees

The statute does not prevent traditional employment arrangements58 if the employee has a bona fide employment relationship with the employer.59 The term "employee" has the same meaning for purposes of satisfying the safe harbor as it has for federal employment tax purposes. Therefore, independent contractor arrangements ordinarily are not safe harbored

56 42 C.F.R. § 1001.952(e).
57 42 C.F.R. § 1001.952(e)(2).
58 See 24 U.S.C. § 3121(d)(2).
59 42 C.F.R. § 1001.952(i).

unless structured to qualify under the personal and management services safe harbor. Under this provision an employee may be, for example, paid on a percentage commission basis for sales of medical supplies, whereas the same arrangements with independent contractors would not be entitled to safe harbor protection.

6) Practitioner Recruitment in Underserved Areas

There is a safe harbor for a recruitment payment by an entity to a physician who has been practicing his or her current specialty for less than one year. The purpose of the payment must be to induce the physician to relocate his or her primary practice place into a health professional shortage area for such specialty that is served by the entity. Under these circumstances, a payment is acceptable if the following requirements are met:[60]

(a) The recruitment benefits must be set out in writing and specify each respective party's obligations;

(b) At least 75% of the revenues must be generated from patients residing in a health professional shortage area or a medically underserved area;

(c) If the physician is leaving an existing practice, at least 75% of the revenues of the new practice must be generated from new patients not previously seen by the physician at his or her former practice;

(d) The period of the arrangement cannot exceed three years;

(e) The arrangement must not require the physician to refer or generate business for the hospital; however, the hospital may require the physician to maintain staff privileges.

(f) The physician may not be restricted as to which hospitals he or she maintains staff privileges;

(g) The benefits provided to the physician must not be determined or based on the value of the volume of expected referrals to the hospital or business generated for the hospital;

(h) The physician must agree to treat Medicare, Medicaid, and any other patients receiving benefits from a federal healthcare program in a nondiscriminatory manner;

(i) Except for the benefit provided to the physician who is being recruited, no other payment or exchange of value may be given to any other person or entity in a position to make or influence referrals.

60 42 C.F.R. § 1001-952(n). According to the preamble to the proposed regulations, the safe harbor does not cover arrangements between hospitals and physicians that are, in reality, payments to obtain the referrals of established practitioners who work, in part, at another hospital in the same area.

7) Investment Interests in Ambulatory Surgical Centers

Four kinds of ambulatory surgical centers ("ASCs") are permitted by the regulations:[61] (i) surgeon-owned; (ii) single-specialty; (iii) multi-specialty; and (iv) hospital/physician. While there are specific requirements for each type of ASC setting, in general, the entity must be Medicare-certified. In addition, the ASC must be a legitimate extension of any physician investor's office practice, and hospital investors cannot make or influence referrals.[62] The Department of Health and Human Services believed that safe harbor protection was warranted for such investment interests because the facility fee to be derived from the procedure done at the ASC is substantially less than the referring physician's professional fee. Thus, this investment interest poses no "significant improper inducement to make referrals."[63]

The following standards must also be met to qualify for the Ambulatory Surgical Center safe harbor:[64]

(i) Investment interests may not be offered on terms related to the previous or expected volume of referrals, services furnished, or amount of business otherwise generated from the investor to the entity;

(ii) One-third (1/3) or more of each physician investor's medical practice income (from all sources) for the previous 12-month period (of the previous fiscal year) must be derived from the physician's performance of ASC procedures;

(iii) The entity or any investor must not loan funds to or guarantee a loan for an investor if the investor uses any part of such loan to obtain the investment interest;

(iv) The amount of payment to an investor in return for the investment must be directly proportional to the amount of the capital investment of that investor;

(v) All ancillary services for Federal health care program beneficiaries performed at the entity must be directly and integrally related to primary procedures performed at the entity, and none may be separately billed to Medicare or other Federal health care programs.

(vi) The entity and any physician investors must treat patients receiving medical benefits or assistance under any Federal health care program in a non-discriminatory manner.

(vii) The ASC must also be a "certified ASC" under federal regulations, its operating and recovery room space must be dedicated exclusively to the ASC, and patients referred to the investment entity must be fully informed of the investor's investment interest.[65] Under these rules, the ASC needs a separate Medicare provider agreement, would need to be licensed by the applicable

61 For the full range of standards applicable to ASCs, see generally 42 C.F.R. Part 416.

62 42 C.F.R. § 1001-952(r).

63 64 Fed. Register 63534 (November 19, 1999).

64 42 C.F.R. § 1001.952(r)(2).

65 42 C.F.R. § 1001.952(r).

state agency (or meet "deemed" status otherwise), and only be able to perform "covered surgical procedures."[66]

42 C.F.R. 1001.952(r) provides the following requirements:

(r) Ambulatory surgical centers. As used in section 1128B of the Act, "remuneration" does not include any payment that is a return on an investment interest, such as a dividend or interest income, made to an investor, as long as the investment entity is a certified ambulatory surgical center (ASC) under part 416 of this title, whose operating and recovery room space is dedicated exclusively to the ASC, patients referred to the investment entity by an investor are fully informed of the investor's investment interest, and all of the applicable standards are met within one of the following four categories—

(1) Surgeon-owned ASCs —If all of the investors are general surgeons or surgeons engaged in the same surgical specialty, who are in a position to refer patients directly to the entity and perform surgery on such referred patients; surgical group practices (as defined in this paragraph) composed exclusively of such surgeons; or investors who are not employed by the entity or by any investor, are not in a position to provide items or services to the entity or any of its investors, and are not in a position to make or influence referrals directly or indirectly to the entity or any of its investors, all of the following six standards must be met—

(i) The terms on which an investment interest is offered to an investor must not be related to the previous or expected volume of referrals, services furnished, or the amount of business otherwise generated from that investor to the entity.

(ii) At least one-third of each surgeon investor's medical practice income from all sources for the previous fiscal year or previous 12-month period must be derived from the surgeon's performance of procedures (as defined in this paragraph).

(iii) The entity or any investor (or other individual or entity acting on behalf of the entity or any investor) must not loan funds to or guarantee a loan for an investor if the investor uses any part of such loan to obtain the investment interest.

(iv) The amount of payment to an investor in return for the investment must be directly proportional to the amount of the capital investment (including the fair market value of any pre-operational services rendered) of that investor.

(v) All ancillary services for Federal health care program beneficiaries performed at the entity must be directly and integrally related to primary procedures performed at the entity, and none may be separately billed to Medicare or other Federal health care programs.

(vi) The entity and any physician investors must treat patients receiving medical benefits or assistance under any Federal health care program in a non-discriminatory manner.

66 42 C.F.R. §§ 416.2, 416.25, 416.65.

(3) Multi-Specialty ASCs —If all of the investors are physicians who are in a position to refer patients directly to the entity and perform procedures on such referred patients; group practices, as defined in this paragraph, composed exclusively of such physicians; or investors who are not employed by the entity or by any investor, are not in a position to provide items or services to the entity or any of its investors, and are not in a position to make or influence referrals directly or indirectly to the entity or any of its investors, all of the following seven standards must be met—

(i) The terms on which an investment interest is offered to an investor must not be related to the previous or expected volume of referals, services furnished, or the amount of business otherwise generated from that investor to the entity.

(ii) At least one-third of each physician investor's medical practice income from all sources for the previous fiscal year or previous 12-month period must be derived from the physician's performance of procedures (as defined in this paragraph).

(iii) At least one-third of the procedures (as defined in this paragraph) performed by each physician investor for the previous fiscal year or previous 12-month period must be performed at the investment entity.

(iv) The entity or any investor (or other individual or entity acting on behalf of the entity or any investor) must not loan funds to or guarantee a loan for an investor if the investor uses any part of such loan to obtain the investment interest.

(v) The amount of payment to an investor in return for the investment must be directly proportional to the amount of the capital investment (including the fair market value of any pre-operational services rendered) of that investor.

(vi) All ancillary services for Federal health care program beneficiaries performed at the entity must be directly and integrally related to primary procedures performed at the entity, and none may be separately billed to Medicare or other Federal health care programs.

(vii) The entity and any physician investors must treat patients receiving medical benefits or assistance under any Federal health care program in a nondiscriminatory manner.

(4) Hospital/Physician ASCs —If at least one investor is a hospital, and all of the remaining investors are physicians who meet the requirements of paragraphs (r)(1), (r)(2) or (r)(3) of this section; group practices (as defined in this paragraph) composed of such physicians; surgical group practices (as defined in this paragraph); or investors who are not employed by the entity or by any investor, are not in a position to provide items or

services to the entity or any of its investors, and are not in a position to refer patients directly or indirectly to the entity or any of its investors, all of the following eight standards must be met—

(viii) The hospital may not be in a position to make or influence referrals directly or indirectly to any investor or the entity.

(5) For purposes of paragraph (r) of this section, procedures means any procedure or procedures on the list of Medicare-covered procedures for ambulatory surgical centers in accordance with regulations issued by the Department and group practice means a group practice that meets all of the standards of paragraph (p) of this section. Surgical group practice means a group practice that meets all of the standards of paragraph (p) of this section and is composed exclusively of surgeons who meet the requirements of paragraph (r)(1) of this section.

8) Referral Agreements for Specialty Services

This safe harbor protects providers who refer a patient back and forth between each other. The safe harbor applies as long as the referrals are medically based, and the physicians do not split a global fee from a federal program for the patient's care.[67] For example, if a non-invasive cardiologist refers a patient to an invasive cardiologist and the invasive cardiologist sends the patient back to see the non-invasive cardiologist after the procedure, this is protected under the law if the two cardiologists are not in the same group practice and share a nuclear scanner or treadmill machine if Medicare pays both of them for the technical component of the tests. It would not be protected if, for example, the patient has an echocardiogram and/or physician bills the technical component and the other bills the professional component of the same test. Unless the parties to the arrangement belong to the same group practice, the only "exchange of value" is the remuneration the parties receive from a third-party payor or the patient for services furnished to the patient.

67 42 C.F.R. § 1001.952(s).

CHAPTER 4
RESTRICTION RELIEF FOR MEDICARE ACCOUNTABLE CARE ORGANIZATIONS ("ACOs")

A. SUMMARY

The Affordable Care Act introduced the Accountable Care Organization. Regulations have been published that provide waivers of federal Anti-Kickback, Stark Law and gain sharing prohibitions within the context of properly organized and operated CMS approved Accountable Care Organizations. Accountable Care Organizations permit participants to be paid fee-for-service Medicare rates for patients while also being indirectly rewarded by virtue the Accountable Care Organization participation if overall patient satisfaction and costs meet certain benchmarks.

With respect to compensation received by a physician (as either an employee or independent contractor) that is derived from his/her participation in an Accountable Care Organization (ACO), the Centers for Medicaid and Medicare Services (CMS) and the Office of Inspector General (OIG) have published five "safe harbors" that waive the compensation restrictions imposed by Stark, the Anti-Kickback Statute, and certain provisions of the Civil Monetary Penalty Law (both Gainsharing and Beneficiary inducements).

These waivers do not apply to any activity that occurs outside of the ACO.

B. ACO WAIVER SPECIFICS

1. "Pre-Participation" Waiver:

This safe harbor waives Stark, the Anti-Kickback Statute, and the Gainsharing Civil Monetary Penalty with respect to financial arrangements that are entered into in anticipation of the ACO's participation agreement with CMS.

2. Shared Savings Distribution Waiver:

This safe harbor waives Stark, the Anti-Kickback Statute, and the Gainsharing Civil Monetary Penalty with respect to distributions or use of shared savings the ACO earns, subject to the following conditions:

i. The ACO has entered into a participation agreement with CMS and remains in good standing under that agreement.

ii. The ACO earned the shared savings.

iii. The ACO earned the shared savings during the term of its participation agreement.

iv. The shared savings are either:

a. distributed to or among the ACO's participants, providers/suppliers, or individuals and entities that were participants or providers/suppliers during the year in which the ACO earned the shared savings; or

b. used for activities that are reasonably related to the purposes of the SSP; and

c. payments of shared savings distributions made directly or indirectly from a hospital to a physician are not made knowingly to induce the physician to reduce or limit medically necessary items or services to patients under the direct care of the physician.

3. Stark Compliance Waiver

The Stark Compliance safe harbor waives the Stark Law's referral prohibitions with respect to any financial relationship between or among the ACO, its participants, and its providers/suppliers, which implicates and fully complies with Stark, subject to three conditions:

i. The ACO has entered into a participation agreement and remains in good standing under that agreement;

ii. The financial relationship is "reasonably related" to the purposes of the ACO program; and

iii. The financial relationship fully complies with a Stark exception.

4. Participation Waiver

This safe harbor waives Stark, the Anti-Kickback Statute, and the Gainsharing Civil Monetary Penalties with respect to any arrangement of an ACO, one or more of its ACO participations or providers/suppliers, or a combination thereof, subject to five conditions:

i. The ACO has entered into a participation agreement and remains in good standing under that agreement;

ii. The ACO meets the requirements concerning ACO governance, leadership, and management;

iii. The ACO's governing body has made and duly authorized a bona fide determination that the arrangement is reasonably related to the purposes of the ACO program;

iv. The party or parties to the arrangement must maintain contemporaneous documentation of the arrangement and authorizations; and

iv. The description of the arrangement must be publicly disclosed at a time and in a place and manner established in guidance issued by CMS.

5. Waiver for Patient Incentives

This safe harbor waives application of the Beneficiary Inducement Civil Monetary Penalty and the Anti-Kickback Statute for items or services provided by an ACO, its ACO participants, or its ACO providers/suppliers to beneficiaries for free or below fair-market value if the following four conditions are all met:

i. The ACO has entered into a participation agreement for the MSSP and remains in good standing thereunder.

ii. There is a reasonable connection between the items or services and medical care of the beneficiary.

iii. The items or services are in-kind.

iv. The items or services are preventive care, or advance one or more of the following clinical goals: Adherence to a treatment regime Adherence to a drug requirement Adherence to a follow-up care plan Management of a chronic disease or condition.

CHAPTER 5
OFFICE OF INSPECTOR GENERAL ROADMAP FOR NEW PHYSICIANS

The Office of the Inspector General is the criminal prosecution arm of Medicare (CMS), and every year hundreds of physicians are investigated for possible criminal action.

The following Roadmap for New Physicians - Avoiding Medicare and Medicaid Fraud and Abuse publication, which includes a hotline that you or your staff can call to turn providers in, is provided in the following pages.

A Roadmap for New Physicians
Avoiding Medicare and
Medicaid Fraud and Abuse
U.S. Department of Health & Human Services
Office of Inspector General

Table of Contents

Introduction

Most physicians strive to work ethically, render high-quality medical care to their patients, and submit proper claims for payment. Society places enormous trust in physicians, and rightly so. Trust is at the core of the physician-patient relationship. When our health is at its most vulnerable, we rely on physicians to use their expert medical training to put us on the road to a healthy recovery.

The Federal Government also places enormous trust in physicians. Medicare, Medicaid, and other Federal health care programs rely on physicians' medical judgment to treat beneficiaries with appropriate services. When reimbursing physicians and hospitals for services provided to program beneficiaries, the Federal Government relies on physicians to submit accurate and truthful claims information.

The presence of some dishonest health care providers who exploit the health care system for illegal personal gain has created the need for laws that combat fraud and abuse and ensure appropriate quality medical care. This brochure assists physicians in understanding how to comply with these Federal laws by identifying "red flags" that could lead to potential liability in law enforcement and administrative actions. The information is organized around three types of relationships that physicians frequently encounter in their careers:

I. Relationships with payers,

II. Relationships with fellow physicians and other providers, and

III. Relationships with vendors.

The key issues addressed in this brochure are relevant to all physicians, regardless of specialty or practice setting.

Fraud and Abuse Laws

The five most important Federal fraud and abuse laws that apply to physicians are the False Claims Act (FCA), the Anti-Kickback Statute (AKS), the Physician Self-Referral Law (Stark law), the Exclusion Authorities, and the Civil Monetary Penalties Law (CMPL). Government agencies, including the Department of Justice, the Department of Health & Human Services Office of Inspector General (OIG), and the Centers for Medicare & Medicaid Services (CMS), are charged with enforcing these laws. As you begin your career, it is crucial to understand these laws not only because following them is the right thing to do, but also because violating them could result in criminal penalties, civil fines, exclusion from the Federal health care programs, or loss of your medical license from your State medical board.

False Claims Act [31 U.S.C. §§ 3729–3733]

The civil FCA protects the Government from being overcharged or sold shoddy goods or services. **It is illegal to submit claims for payment to Medicare or Medicaid that you know or should know are false or fraudulent.** Filing false claims may result in fines of up to three times the programs' loss plus $11,000 per claim filed. Under the civil FCA, each instance of an item or a service billed to Medicare or Medicaid counts as a claim, so fines can add up quickly. The fact that a claim results from a kickback or is made in violation of the Stark law also may render it false or fraudulent, creating liability under the civil FCA as well as the AKS or Stark law.

Under the civil FCA, no specific intent to defraud is required. The civil FCA defines "knowing" to include not only actual knowledge but also instances in which the person acted in deliberate ignorance or reckless disregard of the truth or falsity of the information. Further, the civil FCA contains a whistleblower provision that allows a private individual to file a lawsuit on behalf of the United States and entitles that whistleblower to a percentage of any recoveries. Whistleblowers could be current or ex-business partners, hospital or office staff, patients, or competitors.

There also is a criminal FCA (18 U.S.C. § 287). Criminal penalties for submitting false claims include imprisonment and criminal fines. Physicians have gone to prison for submitting false health care claims. OIG also may impose administrative civil monetary penalties for false or fraudulent claims, as discussed below.

Anti-Kickback Statute [42 U.S.C. § 1320a-7b(b)]

The AKS is a criminal law that prohibits the knowing and willful payment of "remuneration" to induce or reward patient referrals or the generation of business involving any item or service payable by the Federal health care programs (*e.g.*, drugs, supplies, or health care services for Medicare or Medicaid patients). Remuneration includes anything of value and can take many forms besides cash, such as free rent, expensive hotel stays and meals, and excessive compensation for medical directorships or consultancies. **In some industries, it is acceptable to reward those who refer business to you. However, in the Federal health care programs, paying for referrals is a crime.** The statute covers the payers of kickbacks—those who offer or pay remuneration—as well as the recipients of kickbacks—those who solicit or receive remuneration. Each party's intent is a key element of their liability under the AKS.

Criminal penalties and administrative sanctions for violating the AKS include fines, jail terms, and exclusion from participation in the Federal health care programs. Under the CMPL, physicians who pay or accept kickbacks also face penalties of up to $50,000 per kickback plus three times the amount of the remuneration.

Safe harbors protect certain payment and business practices that could otherwise implicate the AKS from criminal and civil prosecution. To be protected by a safe harbor, an arrangement must fit squarely in the safe harbor and satisfy all of its requirements. Some safe harbors address personal services and rental agreements, investments in ambulatory surgical centers, and payments to *bona fide* employees.

For additional information on safe harbors, see "OIG's Safe Harbor Regulations" available at http://oig.hhs.gov/fraud/safeharborregulations.asp.

As a physician, you are an attractive target for kickback schemes because you can be a source of referrals for fellow physicians or other health care providers and suppliers. You decide what drugs your patients use, which specialists they see, and what health care services and supplies they receive.

Many people and companies want your patients' business and would pay you to send that business their way. Just as it is illegal for you to take money from providers and suppliers in return for the referral of your Medicare and Medicaid patients, it is illegal for you to pay others to refer their Medicare and Medicaid patients to you.

Kickbacks in health care can lead to:

- Overutilization
- Increased program costs
- Corruption of medical decisionmaking
- Patient steering
- Unfair competition

The kickback prohibition applies to all sources of referrals, even patients. For example, where the Medicare and Medicaid programs require patients to pay copays for services, you are generally required to collect that money from your patients. Routinely waiving these copays could implicate the AKS and you may not advertise that you will forgive copayments. However, you are free to waive a copayment if you make an individual determination that the patient cannot afford to pay or if your reasonable collection efforts fail. **It is also legal to provide free or discounted services to uninsured people.**

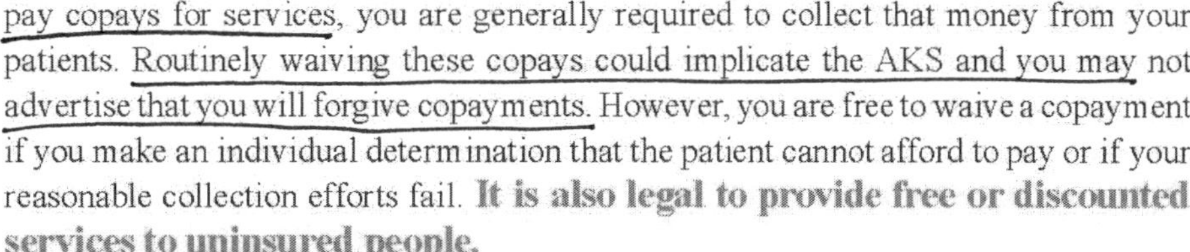

Besides the AKS, the beneficiary inducement statute (42 U.S.C. § 1320a-7a(a)(5)) also imposes civil monetary penalties on physicians who offer remuneration to Medicare and Medicaid beneficiaries to influence them to use their services.

The Government does not need to prove patient harm or financial loss to the programs to show that a physician violated the AKS. A physician can be guilty of violating the AKS even if the physician actually rendered the service and the service was medically necessary. **Taking money or gifts from a drug or device company or a durable medical equipment (DME) supplier is not justified by the argument that you would have prescribed that drug or ordered that wheelchair even without a kickback.**

Physician Self-Referral Law [42 U.S.C. § 1395nn]

The Physician Self-Referral Law, commonly referred to as the Stark law, prohibits physicians from referring patients to receive "designated health services" payable by Medicare or Medicaid from entities with which the physician or an immediate family member has a financial relationship, unless an exception applies. Financial relationships include both ownership/investment interests and compensation arrangements. For example, if you invest in an imaging center, the Stark law requires the resulting financial relationship to fit within an exception or you may not refer patients to the facility and the entity may not bill for the referred imaging services.

"Designated health services" are:

- clinical laboratory services;
- physical therapy, occupational therapy, and outpatient speech-language pathology services;
- radiology and certain other imaging services;
- radiation therapy services and supplies;
- DME and supplies;
- parenteral and enteral nutrients, equipment, and supplies;
- prosthetics, orthotics, and prosthetic devices and supplies;
- home health services;
- outpatient prescription drugs; and
- inpatient and outpatient hospital services.

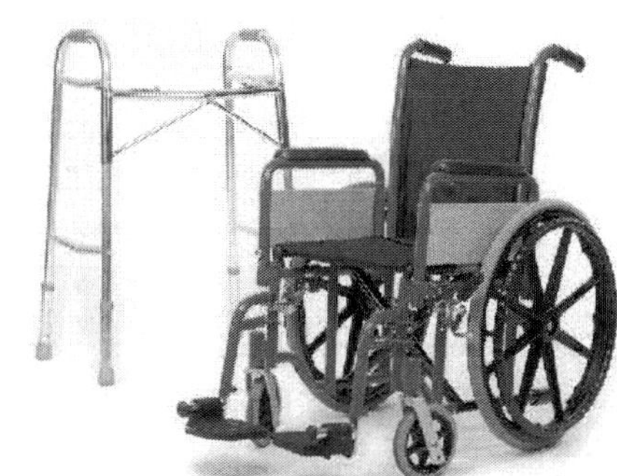

The Stark law is a strict liability statute, which means proof of specific intent to violate the law is not required. The Stark law prohibits the submission, or causing the submission, of claims in violation of the law's restrictions on referrals. Penalties for physicians who violate the Stark law include fines as well as exclusion from participation in the Federal health care programs.

For more information, see CMS's Stark law Web site available at http://www.cms.gov/physicianselfreferral/.

Exclusion Statute [42 U.S.C. § 1320a-7]

OIG is legally required to exclude from participation in all Federal health care programs individuals and entities convicted of the following types of criminal offenses: (1) Medicare or Medicaid fraud, as well as any other offenses related to the delivery of items or services under Medicare or Medicaid; (2) patient abuse or neglect; (3) felony convictions for other health-care-related fraud, theft, or other financial misconduct; and (4) felony convictions for unlawful manufacture, distribution, prescription, or dispensing of controlled substances. OIG has discretion to exclude individuals and entities on several other grounds, including misdemeanor convictions related to health care fraud other than Medicare or Medicaid fraud or misdemeanor convictions in connection with the unlawful manufacture, distribution, prescription, or dispensing of controlled substances; suspension, revocation, or surrender of a license to provide health care for reasons bearing on professional competence, professional performance, or financial integrity; provision of unnecessary or substandard services; submission of false or fraudulent claims to a Federal health care program; engaging in unlawful kickback arrangements; and defaulting on health education loan or scholarship obligations.

If you are excluded by OIG from participation in the Federal health care programs, then Medicare, Medicaid, and other Federal health care programs, such as TRICARE and the Veterans Health Administration, will not pay for items or services that you furnish, order, or prescribe. **Excluded physicians may not bill directly for treating Medicare and Medicaid patients, nor may their services be billed indirectly through an employer or a group practice.** In addition, if you furnish services to a patient on a private-pay basis, no order or prescription that you give to that patient will be reimbursable by any Federal health care program.

For more information, see OIG's Special Advisory Bulletin entitled "The Effect of Exclusion From Participation in Federal Health Care Programs" available at http://oig.hhs.gov/fraud/docs/alertsandbulletins/effected.htm.

You are responsible for ensuring that you do not employ or contract with excluded individuals or entities, whether in a physician practice, a clinic, or in any capacity or setting in which Federal health care programs may reimburse for the items or services furnished by those employees or contractors. This responsibility requires screening all current and prospective employees and contractors against OIG's List of Excluded Individuals and Entities. This online database can be accessed from OIG's Exclusion Web site. If you employ or contract with an excluded individual or entity and Federal health care program payment is made for items or services that person or entity furnishes, whether directly or indirectly, you may be subject to a civil monetary penalty and/or an obligation to repay any amounts attributable to the services of the excluded individual or entity.

For more information, see OIG's exclusion Web site available at http://oig.hhs.gov/fraud/exclusions.asp.

Civil Monetary Penalties Law [42 U.S.C. § 1320a-7a]

OIG may seek civil monetary penalties and sometimes exclusion for a wide variety of conduct and is authorized to seek different amounts of penalties and assessments based on the type of violation at issue. Penalties range from $10,000 to $50,000 per violation. Some examples of CMPL violations include:

- presenting a claim that the person knows or should know is for an item or service that was not provided as claimed or is false or fraudulent;
- presenting a claim that the person knows or should know is for an item or service for which payment may not be made;
- violating the AKS;
- violating Medicare assignment provisions;
- violating the Medicare physician agreement;
- providing false or misleading information expected to influence a decision to discharge;
- failing to provide an adequate medical screening examination for patients who present to a hospital emergency department with an emergency medical condition or in labor; and
- making false statements or misrepresentations on applications or contracts to participate in the Federal health care programs.

I. Physician Relationships With Payers

During residency, you probably are not focused on who pays for your patients' care. Once you start practicing, it is important to understand who the payers are. The U.S. health care system relies heavily on third-party payers, and, therefore, your patients often are not the ones who pay most of their medical bills. Third-party payers include commercial insurers and the Federal and State governments. **When the Federal Government covers items or services rendered to Medicare and Medicaid beneficiaries, the Federal fraud and abuse laws apply.** Many States also have adopted similar laws that apply to your provision of care under State-financed programs and to private-pay patients. Consequently, you should recognize that the issues discussed here may apply to your care of all insured patients.

Accurate Coding and Billing

Payers trust you, as a physician, to provide necessary, cost-effective, and quality care. You exert significant influence over what services your patients receive, you control the documentation describing what services they actually received, and your documentation serves as the basis for bills sent to insurers for services you provided. The Government's payment of claims is generally based solely on your representations in the claims documents.

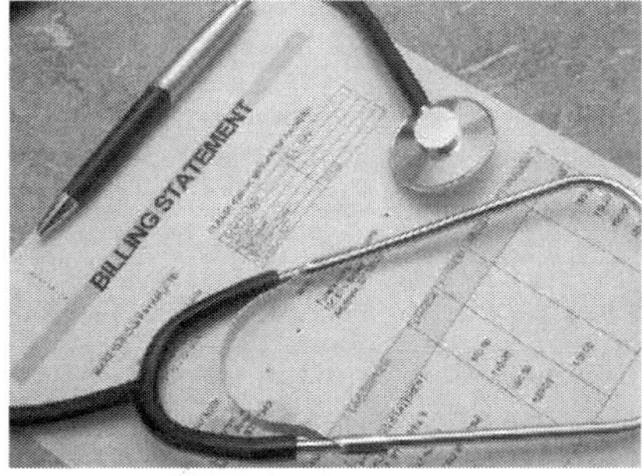

Because the Government invests so much trust in physicians on the front end, Congress provided powerful criminal, civil, and administrative enforcement tools for instances when unscrupulous providers abuse that trust. The Government has broad capabilities to audit claims and investigate providers when it has a reason to suspect fraud. Suspicion of fraud and abuse may be raised by irregular billing patterns or reports from others, including your staff, competitors, and patients.

When you submit a claim for services performed for a Medicare or Medicaid beneficiary, you are filing a bill with the Federal Government and certifying that you have earned the payment requested and complied with the billing requirements. If you knew or should have known that the submitted claim was false, then the attempt to collect unearned money constitutes a violation. A common type of false claim is "upcoding," which refers to using billing codes that reflect a more severe illness than actually existed or a more expensive treatment than was provided. Additional examples of improper claims include:

- billing for services that you did not actually render;
- billing for services that were not medically necessary;
- billing for services that were performed by an improperly supervised or unqualified employee;
- billing for services that were performed by an employee who has been excluded from participation in the Federal health care programs;
- billing for services of such low quality that they are virtually worthless; and

- billing separately for services already included in a global fee, like billing for an evaluation and management service the day after surgery.

CAUTION CAUTION CAUTION CAUTION CAUTION CAUTION CAUTION

Upcoding

Medicare pays for many physician services using Evaluation and Management (commonly referred to as "E&M") codes. New patient visits generally require more time than follow-up visits for established patients, and therefore E&M codes for new patients command higher reimbursement rates than E&M codes for established patients. An example of upcoding is an instance when you provide a follow-up office visit or follow-up inpatient consultation but bill using a higher level E&M code as if you had provided a comprehensive new patient office visit or an initial inpatient consultation.

Another example of upcoding related to E&M codes is misuse of Modifier 25. Modifier 25 allows additional payment for a separate E&M service rendered on the same day as a procedure. Upcoding occurs if a provider uses Modifier 25 to claim payment for an E&M service when the patient care rendered was not significant, was not separately identifiable, and was not above and beyond the care usually associated with the procedure.

CAUTION CAUTION CAUTION CAUTION CAUTION CAUTION CAUTION

Case Examples of Fraudulent Billing

• A psychiatrist was fined $400,000 and permanently excluded from participating in the Federal health care programs for misrepresenting that he provided therapy sessions requiring 30 or 60 minutes of face-to-face time with the patient, when he had provided only medication checks for 15 minutes or less. The psychiatrist also misrepresented that he provided therapy sessions when in fact a non-licensed individual conducted the sessions.

• A dermatologist was sentenced to 2 years of probation and 6 months of home confinement and ordered to pay $2.9 million after he pled guilty to one count of obstruction of a criminal health care fraud investigation. The dermatologist admitted to falsifying lab tests and backdating letters to referring physicians to substantiate false diagnoses to make the documentation appear that his patients had Medicare-covered conditions when they did not.

• A cardiologist paid the Government $435,000 and entered into a 5-year Integrity Agreement with OIG to settle allegations that he knowingly submitted claims for consultation services that were not supported by patient medical records and did not meet the criteria for a consultation. The physician also allegedly knowingly submitted false claims for E&M services when he had already received payment for such services in connection with previous claims for nuclear stress testing.

• An endocrinologist billed routine blood draws as critical care blood draws. He paid $447,000 to settle allegations of upcoding and other billing violations.

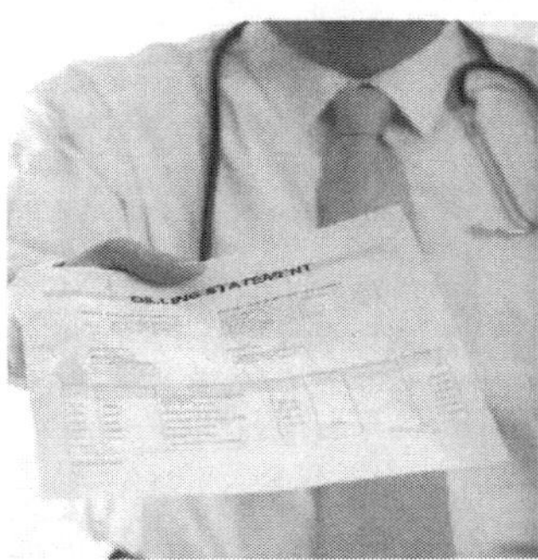

11

Physician Documentation

Physicians should maintain accurate and complete medical records and documentation of the services they provide. Physicians also should ensure that the claims they submit for payment are supported by the documentation. The Medicare and Medicaid programs may review beneficiaries' medical records. **Good documentation practice helps ensure that your patients receive appropriate care from you and other providers who may rely on your records for patients' past medical histories.** It also helps you address challenges raised against the integrity of your bills. You may have heard the saying regarding malpractice litigation: "If you didn't document it, it's the same as if you didn't do it." The same can be said for Medicare and Medicaid billing.

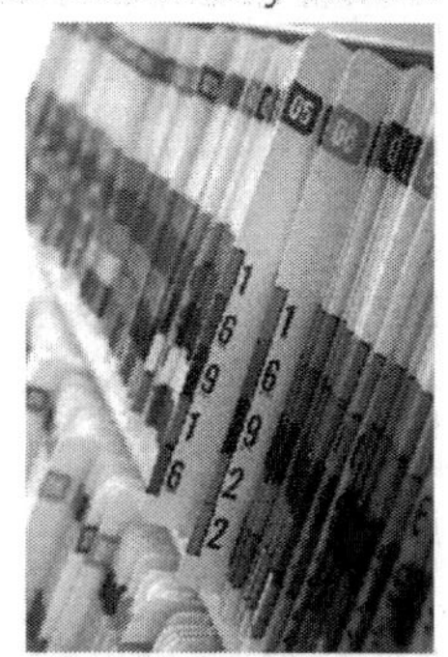

For more information on physician documentation, see CMS's Documentation Guidelines for Evaluation and Management Services available at http://www.cms.gov/MLNEdWebGuide/25_EMDOC.asp.

Enrolling as a Medicare and Medicaid Provider With CMS

CMS is the Federal agency that administers the Medicare program and monitors the Medicaid programs run by each State. To obtain reimbursement from the Government for services provided to Federal health care program beneficiaries, you must:

1. **Obtain a National Provider Identifier (NPI).** An NPI is a unique health identifier for health care providers. You may apply for your NPI at https://nppes.cms.hhs.gov/NPPES/Welcome.do.
2. **Complete the appropriate Medicare Enrollment Application.** During the enrollment process, CMS collects information to ensure that you are qualified and eligible to enroll in the Medicare Program. Information about Medicare provider enrollment is available at http://www.cms.gov/MedicareProviderSupEnroll/.
3. **Complete your State-specific Medicaid Enrollment Application.** Information about Medicaid provider enrollment is available from your State Medicaid agency.

Once you become a Medicare and/or Medicaid provider, you are responsible for ensuring that claims submitted under your number are true and correct.

For tips you can share with your patients on how they can protect themselves from medical identity theft, see OIG's brochure entitled "Tips to Avoid Medical ID Theft" available at http://oig.hhs.gov/fraud/IDTheft/OIG_Medical_Identity_Theft_Brochure.pdf.

Prescription Authority

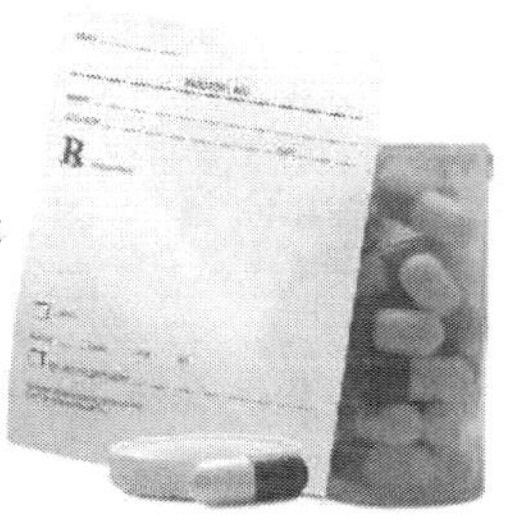

The Drug Enforcement Administration (DEA) is a Department of Justice agency responsible for enforcing the Controlled Substances Act. When you prepare to enter practice, you probably will apply for a DEA number that authorizes you to write prescriptions for controlled substances. You also will apply for your State medical license and any additional credentials your State requires for you to write prescriptions. You must ensure that you write prescriptions only for lawful purposes.

Case Examples of Misuse of Physician Provider and Prescription Numbers

- A physician was ordered to pay $50,000 in restitution to the Government for falsely indicating on his provider number application that he was running his own practice when, in fact, a neurophysiologist was operating the practice and paying the physician a salary for the use of his number.

- An osteopathic physician was sentenced to 10 years in prison and ordered to pay $7.9 million in restitution after she accepted cash payments for signing preprinted prescriptions and Certificates of Medical Necessity for motorized wheelchairs for beneficiaries she never examined. More than 60 DME companies received Medicare and Medicaid payments based on her fraudulent prescriptions.

- An internal medicine physician pled guilty to Medicare fraud and to conspiring to dispense oxycodone, morphine, hydrocodone, and alprazolam. The physician allowed unauthorized and non-medical employees at his pain center to prescribe drugs using his pre-signed blank prescription forms. Prescriptions were issued in his name without adequate physical exams, proper diagnoses, or consideration of alternative treatment options. He paid $317,000 in restitution to the Government.

Assignment Issues in Medicare Reimbursement

Most physicians bill Medicare as participating providers, which is referred to as "accepting assignment." Each year, Medicare promulgates a fee schedule setting the reimbursement for each physician service. Once beneficiaries satisfy their annual deductible, Medicare pays 80 percent of the fee schedule amount and the beneficiary pays 20 percent. Participating providers receive the Medicare program's 80 percent directly from the Medicare program and bill the beneficiary for the remaining 20 percent. Accepting assignment means that the physician accepts the Medicare payment plus any copayment or deductible Medicare requires the patient to pay *as the full payment for the physician's services and that the physician will not seek any extra payment* (beyond the copayment or deductible) from the patient. Medicare participating physicians may not bill Medicare patients extra for services that are already covered by Medicare. Doing so is a violation of a physician's assignment agreement and can lead to penalties.

The second, less common, way to obtain Medicare reimbursement is to bill as a non-participating provider. Non-participating providers do not receive direct payment from the Medicare program. Rather, they bill their patients and the patients seek reimbursement from Medicare. Although non-participating providers are not subject to the assignment rules, they still must limit the dollar amount of their charges to Medicare patients. Generally, non-participating providers may not charge Medicare beneficiaries more than 15 percent in excess of the Medicare fee schedule amount. It is illegal to charge patients more than the limiting charge established for physicians' services.

Excluded providers may not receive Medicare payment either as participating or non-participating providers.

You may see advertisements offering to help you convert your practice into a "boutique," "concierge," or "retainer" practice. Many such solicitations promise to help you work less, yet earn more money. **If you are a participating or non-participating physician, you may not ask Medicare patients to pay a second time for services for which Medicare has already paid.** It is legal to charge patients for services that are not covered by Medicare. However, charging an "access fee" or "administrative fee" that simply allows them to obtain Medicare-covered services from your practice constitutes double billing.

Case Example of a Physician Violating an Assignment Agreement by Charging Beneficiaries Extra Fees

- A physician paid $107,000 to resolve potential liability for charging patients, including Medicare beneficiaries, an annual fee. In exchange for the fee, the physician offered: (1) an annual physical; (2) same- or next-day appointments; (3) dedicated support personnel; (4) around-the-clock physician availability; (5) prescription facilitation; (6) expedited and coordinated referrals; and (7) other amenities at the physician's discretion. The physician's activities allegedly violated the assignment agreement because some of the services outlined in the annual fee were already covered by Medicare.

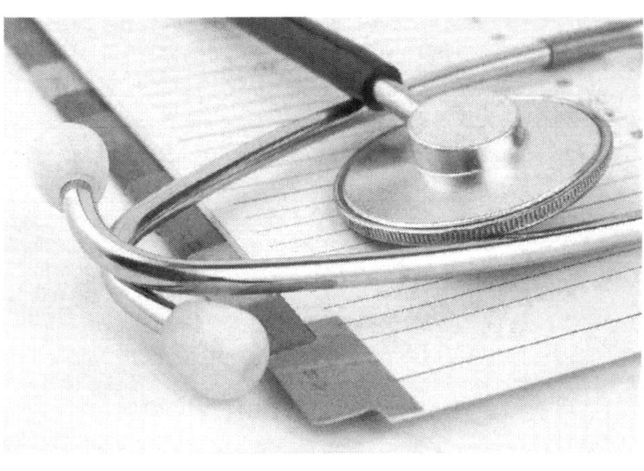

II. Physician Relationships With Fellow Providers: Physicians, Hospitals, Nursing Homes, Etc.

Any time a health care business offers something to you for free or at below fair market value, you always should ask yourself, "*Why?*" For example, if a DME supplier offers to give you cash or to pay for your summer vacation, you should suspect that the supplier is trying to induce you to refer your patients to that vendor. If a laboratory offers to decorate your patient waiting room, you should suspect that it is trying to induce you to send your lab business its way.

For more information on physician relationships with:

fellow providers, see OIG's "Compliance Program Guidance for Individual and Small Group Physician Practices" available at http://oig.hhs.gov/authorities/docs/physician.pdf;

hospitals, see OIG's "Supplemental Compliance Program Guidance for Hospitals" available at http://oig.hhs.gov/fraud/docs/complianceguidance/012705HospSupplementalGuidance.pdf; and

nursing homes, see OIG's "Supplemental Compliance Program Guidance for Nursing Facilities" available at http://oig.hhs.gov/fraud/docs/complianceguidance/nhg_fr.pdf.

Physician Investments in Health Care Business Ventures

Some have observed that physicians who invest in health care business ventures with outside parties (*e.g.*, imaging centers, labs, equipment vendors, or physical therapy clinics) refer more patients for the services provided by those parties than physicians who do not invest. Maybe this disproportionate utilization partly reflects the physicians' belief in the value of the services or technology, prompting the investments in the first place. However, there also is a risk that the physicians' belief in the value of the services or technology is less a cause than an effect of the investment interest. The physician investors' disproportionate utilization may be motivated partly by the physicians' ability to profit from the use of the ancillary services. These business relationships can sometimes unduly influence or distort physician decisionmaking and result in the improper steering of a patient to a particular therapy or source of services in which a physician has a financial interest. **Excessive and medically unnecessary referrals waste Government and beneficiary money and**

can expose beneficiaries to harm from unnecessary services. Many of these investment relationships have serious legal risks under the AKS and Stark law.

If you are invited to invest in a health care business whose products you might order or to which you might refer your patients, you should ask the following questions. If the answer is "yes" to any of them, you should consider carefully whether you are investing for legitimate reasons.

- ? Are you being offered an investment interest for a nominal capital contribution?
- ? Will your ownership share be larger than your share of the aggregate capital contributions made to the venture?
- ? Is the venture promising you high rates of return for little or no financial risk?
- ? Is the venture or any potential business partner offering to loan you the money to make your capital contribution?
- ? Are you being asked to promise or guarantee that you will refer patients or order items or services from the venture?
- ? Do you believe you will be more likely to refer more patients for the items and services provided by the venture if you make the investment?
- ? Do you believe you will be more likely to refer to the venture just because you made the investment?
- ? Will the venture have sufficient capital from other sources to fund its ongoing operations?

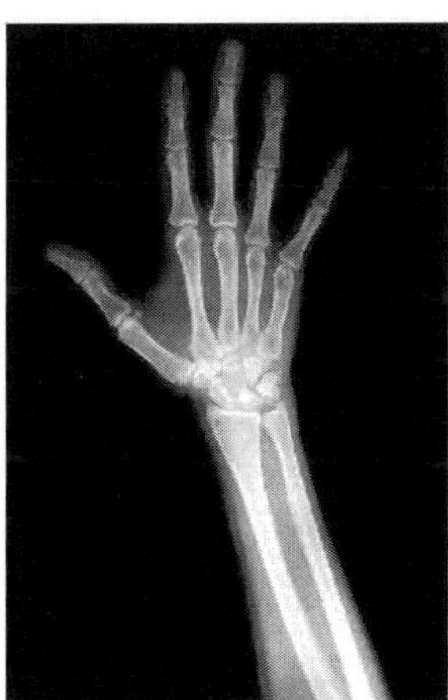

For more information on physician investments, see:

OIG's Special Fraud Alert entitled "Joint Venture Arrangements" available at http://oig.hhs.gov/fraud/docs/alertsandbulletins/121994.html;

OIG's Special Advisory Bulletin on contractual joint ventures available at http://oig.hhs.gov/fraud/docs/alertsandbulletins/042303SABJointVentures.pdf; and

OIG's "Supplemental Compliance Program Guidance for Hospitals" available at http://oig.hhs.gov/fraud/docs/complianceguidance/012705HospSupplementalGuidance.pdf.

Case Examples Involving Kickbacks for Referrals and Self-Referrals

- Nine cardiologists paid the Government over $3.2 million for allegedly engaging in a kickback scheme. The cardiologists received salaries under clinical faculty services agreements with a hospital under which, the Government alleged, they did not provide some or any of the services. In exchange, the cardiologists referred their patients to the hospital for cardiology services. Two of the physicians also pled guilty to criminal embezzlement charges involving the same conduct.

- A physician paid the Government $203,000 to settle allegations that he violated the physician self-referral prohibition in the Stark law for routinely referring Medicare patients to an oxygen supply company he owned.

Physician Recruitment

A hospital will sometimes provide a physician with a recruitment incentive to induce the physician to relocate to the hospital's geographic area, become a member of its medical staff, and establish a practice that helps serve that community's medical needs. Often, such recruitment efforts are legitimately designed to fill a "clinical gap" in a medically underserved area to which it may be difficult to attract physicians in the absence of financial incentives. However, as you begin planning your professional future and perhaps receiving recruitment offers, you need to be aware that in some communities, especially ones with multiple hospitals, the competition for patients can be fierce. Some hospitals may offer illegal inducements to you, or to the established physician practice you join in the hospital's community, to gain referrals. This means that the competition for your loyalty can cross the line into illegal arrangements for which *both you and the hospital* can be liable.

Recruitment arrangements are of special interest to graduating residents and fellows. Within very specific parameters specified in the Stark law and subject to compliance with the AKS, hospitals may provide relocation assistance and practice support under a properly structured recruitment arrangement to assist you in establishing a practice in the hospital's community. Alternatively, a hospital may pay you a fair market value salary as an employee or pay you fair market value for specific services you render to the hospital as an independent contractor. However, the hospital may not offer you money, provide you free or below-market rent for your medical office, or engage in similar activities designed to influence your referral decisions. **You should admit your patients to the hospital best suited to care for their particular medical conditions or to the hospital your patient selects based on his or her preference or insurance coverage.** As noted, if a hospital or physician practice seperately or jointly is recruiting you as a new physician to the community, you may be offered a recruitment package. But, you may not negotiate for benefits in exchange for a promise—implicit or explicit—that you will admit your patients to a specific hospital or practice setting unless you are a hospital employee. You should seek knowledgeable legal counsel if someone with whom you are entering into a relationship requires you to admit patients to a specific hospital or practice group.

Tips for Medical Directors

If you choose to accept a medical directorship at a nursing home or other facility, you must be prepared to assume substantial professional responsibility for the care delivered at the facility. As medical director, patients (both your own patients and the patients of other attending physicians) and their families count on you, and State and Federal authorities may hold you accountable as well. To do this job well, you should:

- actively oversee clinical care in the facility;
- lead the medical staff to meet the standard of care;
- ensure proper training, education, and oversight for physicians, nurses, and other staff members; and
- identify and address quality problems.

Case Examples of Medical Directorship Issues

- A physician group practice paid the Government $1 million and entered into a 5-year Corporate Integrity Agreement to settle alleged violations of the AKS, FCA, and Stark law related to medical directorships with a medical center. Allegedly, the agreements were not in writing, the physicians were paid more than fair market value for the services they rendered, and the payment amounts were based on the value of referrals the physicians sent to the medical center.

- Two orthopedic surgeons paid $450,000 and $250,000 to settle allegations related to improper medical directorships with a company that operated a diagnostic imaging center, a rehabilitation facility, and an ambulatory surgery center. The company allegedly provided the physicians with valuable compensation, including free use of the corporate jet, under the medical directorship agreements, which required the physicians to render limited services in return. The agreements with the physicians allegedly called for redundant services and served to encourage the physicians to refer their patients to the facilities operated by the company.

III. Physician Relationships With Vendors

Free Samples

Some physicians welcome visits from pharmaceutical salespeople, while other physicians prefer not to directly engage with industry representatives. If you decide to make your practice accessible to salespeople, you probably will be offered product samples. Many drug and biologic companies provide physicians with free samples that the physicians may give to patients free of charge. **It is legal to give these samples to your patients for free, but it is illegal to sell the samples.** The Government has prosecuted physicians for billing Medicare for free samples. Opinions differ on whether sampling practices ultimately increase or decrease patients' long-term drug costs. If you choose to accept samples, you will need reliable systems in place to safely store the samples and ensure that samples are not commingled with your commercial stock.

Case Example Involving Drug Samples

- Several urologists pled guilty to charges of conspiracy, paid restitution in the tens of thousands of dollars, and received sanctions against their medical licenses for billing Medicare for injectable prostate cancer drugs they received for free from two pharmaceutical companies. The pharmaceutical companies paid $1.4 billion for their part of the alleged scheme to give urologists free samples and encourage them to bill Medicare at an inflated price. The pharmaceutical companies also provided urologists with additional inducements to use their drugs over the competitor's products, including drug rebates, education grants, volume discounts, free goods, and debt forgiveness.

Relationships With the Pharmaceutical and Medical Device Industries

Physician-industry collaboration can produce important medical advances. However, some pharmaceutical and device companies have used sham consulting agreements and other arrangements to buy physician loyalty to their products. Such illegal arrangements induce physicians to prescribe or use products on the basis of that loyalty to the company or to get more money from the company, rather than because it is the best treatment for the patient.

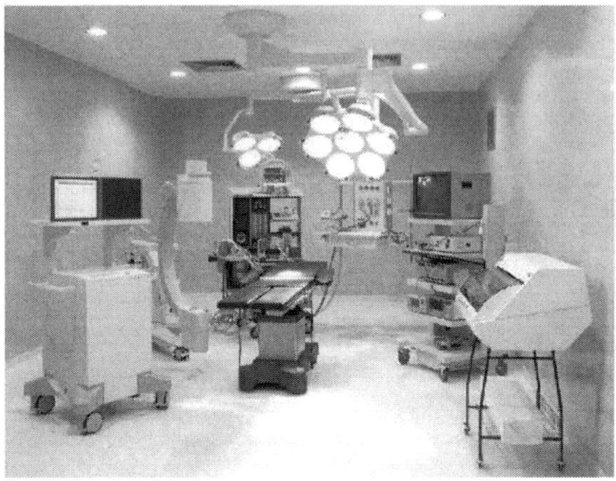

As a practicing physician, you may have opportunities to work as a consultant or promotional speaker for the drug or device industry. For every financial relationship offered to you, evaluate the link between the services you can provide and the compensation you will receive. Test the propriety of any proposed relationship by asking yourself the following questions:

- ? Does the company *really* need *my* particular expertise or input?
- ? Does the amount of money the company is offering seem fair, appropriate, and commercially reasonable for what it is asking me to do?
- ? Is it possible the company is paying me for my loyalty so that I will prescribe its drugs or use its devices?

A good discussion that assists in distinguishing between legitimate and questionable industry relationships is located in the OIG's "Compliance Program Guidance for Pharmaceutical Manufacturers" available at http://oig.hhs.gov/authorities/docs/03/050503FRCPGPharmac.pdf.

If your contribution is your time and effort or your ability to generate useful ideas and the payment you receive is fair market value compensation for your services without regard to referrals, then, depending on the circumstances, you may legitimately serve as a *bona fide* consultant. **If your contribution is your ability to prescribe a drug or use a medical device or refer your patients for particular services or supplies, the proposed consulting arrangement likely is one you should avoid as it could violate fraud and abuse laws.**

For example, if a drug company offers to pay you and a hundred other "thought leaders" to attend a conference in the Bahamas without requiring preparatory work on your part or information about your expertise in the field (other than the fact that you are a licensed physician), you should be suspicious that the company is attempting to influence you to prescribe its drug.

Case Example of Kickbacks in the Device Industry

CASE EXAMPLES

• Four orthopedic device manufacturers paid $311 million to settle kickback and false claims allegations that the companies bribed surgeons to recommend their hip and knee surgical implant products. The companies allegedly would award physicians with vacations, gifts, and annual "consulting fees" as high as $200,000 in return for the physicians' endorsements of their implants or use of them in operations. Many of the individual orthopedic surgeons at the receiving end of the kickbacks are the subject of ongoing investigations by the Government. One orthopedic surgeon recently paid $650,000 to resolve allegations that the surgeon accepted payments from device manufacturers to use their hip and knee implants.

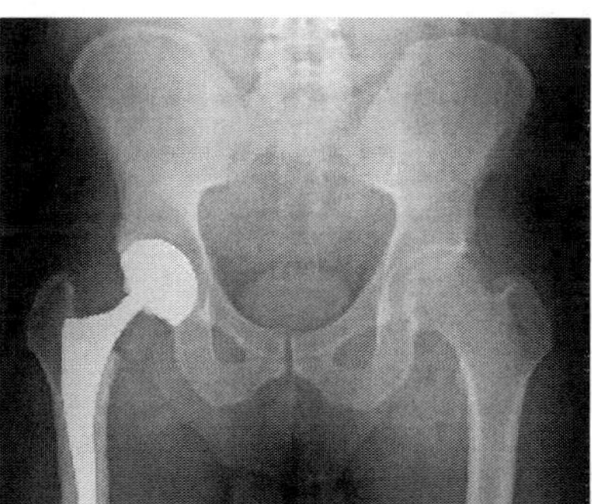

Transparency in Physician-Industry Relationships

Although some physicians believe that free lunches, subsidized trips, and gifts do not affect their medical judgment, research shows that these types of perquisites can influence prescribing practices. Recent pharmaceutical company settlements with the Department of Justice and OIG require "transparency" in physician-industry relationships, whether by requiring the pharmaceutical company to provide the Government with a list of physicians whom the company paid and/or by requiring ongoing public disclosure by the company of physician payments. **The public will soon know what gifts and payments a physician receives from industry.** The Patient Protection and Affordable Care Act of 2010 requires drug, device, and biologic companies to publicly report nearly all gifts or payments they make to physicians beginning in 2013.

Academic institutions also may impose various restrictions on the interactions their faculty members or affiliated physicians have with industry. These and other considerations may factor into your decision about whether you want to conduct industry-sponsored research; serve as a consultant or director for a drug, biologic, or device company; apply for industry-sponsored educational or research grants; or engage in other relationships with industry.

> Both the pharmaceutical industry (through PhRMA) and the medical device industry (through AdvaMed) have adopted codes of ethics for their respective industries regarding relationships with health care professionals. Both codes are available online.

Conflict-of-Interest Disclosures

Many of the relationships discussed in this brochure are subject to conflict-of-interest disclosure policies. Even if the relationships are legal, you may have an obligation to disclose their existence. Rules about disclosing and managing conflicts of interest come from a variety of sources, including grant funders, such as States, universities, and the National Institutes of Health, and from the Food and Drug Administration (FDA) when data are submitted to support marketing approval for new drugs, devices, or biologics. To "manage" your conflicts of interest, consider the conflicts policies that affect your professional activities, candidly disclose any industry money subject to these policies, and adhere to restrictions on your activities. If you are uncertain whether a conflict exists, ask someone. You always can apply the "newspaper test" and ask yourself whether you would want the arrangement to appear on the front page of your local newspaper.

Continuing Medical Education

After finishing your formal graduate medical training, you will assume greater responsibility for your continuing medical education (CME) to maintain State licensure, hospital privileges, and board certification. Drug and device manufacturers sponsor many educational opportunities for physicians. **It is important to distinguish between CME sessions that are educational in nature and sessions that constitute marketing by a drug or device manufacturer.** Industry satellite programs that occur concurrently with a society meeting are generally promotional, even if the primary speaker is a physician who is well known in the field. You should be circumspect about a discussion that focuses on a particular brand drug or device, as opposed to all the treatment alternatives for a specific condition.

For example, if speakers recommend use of a drug to treat conditions for which there is no FDA approval or use of a drug by children when FDA has approved only adult use, you should independently seek out the empirical data that support these recommendations. **Note that although physicians may prescribe drugs for off-label uses, it is illegal under the Federal Food, Drug, and Cosmetic Act for drug manufacturers to promote off-label uses of drugs.**

Advertisements and other promotional materials for drugs, biologics, and medical devices must be truthful, not misleading, and limited to approved uses. FDA is requesting physicians' assistance in identifying misleading advertisements through its Bad Ad Program. If you spot advertising violations, you should report them to FDA by calling 877-RX-DDMAC (877-793-3622) or by emailing badad@fda.gov.

If you are invited to serve as faculty for industry-sponsored CME, ask yourself the following questions:

- ? Does the sponsor *really* need *my* particular expertise or input?
- ? Does the amount of money the sponsor is offering seem fair and appropriate for the educational value I will add to the presentation?
- ? Is it possible the sponsor is paying me for my loyalty so that I will prescribe its drugs or use its devices?
- ? Does the sponsor prepare a slide deck and speaker notes, or am I free to set the content of the lecture?

Compliance Programs for Physicians

Establishing and following a compliance program will help physicians avoid fraudulent activities and ensure that they are submitting true and accurate claims. The following seven components provide a solid basis upon which a physician practice can create a voluntary compliance program:

1. Conduct internal monitoring and auditing.
2. Implement compliance and practice standards.
3. Designate a compliance officer or contact.
4. Conduct appropriate training and education.
5. Respond appropriately to detected offenses and develop corrective action.
6. Develop open lines of communication with employees.
7. Enforce disciplinary standards through well-publicized guidelines.

With the passage of the Patient Protection and Affordable Care Act of 2010, physicians who treat Medicare and Medicaid beneficiaries will be required to establish a compliance program.

For more information on compliance programs for physicians, see OIG's "Compliance Program Guidance for Individual and Small Group Physician Practices" available at http://oig.hhs.gov/authorities/docs/physician.pdf.

Where To Go for Help

When you are considering whether or not to engage in a particular billing practice; enter into a particular business venture; or pursue an employment, consulting, or other personal services relationship, it is prudent to evaluate the arrangement for potential compliance problems. The following is a list of possible resources that can help you.

- Experienced health care lawyers can analyze your issues and provide a legal evaluation and risk analysis of the proposed venture, relationship, or arrangement.

- The Bar Association in your State may have a directory of attorneys in your area who practice in the health care field.
- Your State or local medical society may be a good resource for issues affecting physicians and may have listings of health care lawyers in your area.
- Your specialty society may have information on additional risk areas specific to your type of practice.
- CMS's local contractor medical directors are a valuable source of information on Medicare coverage policies and appropriate billing practices. The contact information for local contractors is available at http://www.cms.gov/MLNGenInfo/30_contactus.asp.
- CMS's "Medicare Physician Guide: A Resource for Residents, Practicing Physicians, and Other Health Care Professionals" available at http://www.cms.gov/MLNProducts/downloads/physicianguide.pdf, provides an overview of the Medicare program and information on Medicare reimbursement and payment policies.
- The OIG's Web site, available at http://oig.hhs.gov, provides substantial fraud and abuse guidance.
- As discussed above, OIG issues Compliance Program Guidance documents that include compliance recommendations and discussions of fraud and abuse risk areas. These guidance documents are available at http://oig.hhs.gov/fraud/complianceguidance.asp.
- OIG issues advisory opinions to parties who seek advice on the application of the AKS, CMPL, and Exclusion Authorities. Information on how to request an OIG advisory opinion and links to previously published OIG advisory opinions are available at http://oig.hhs.gov/fraud/advisoryopinions.asp.
- CMS issues advisory opinions to parties who seek advice on the Stark law. Information on how to request a CMS advisory opinion and links to previously published CMS advisory opinions are available at http://www.cms.gov/PhysicianSelfReferral/95_advisory_opinions.asp.

What To Do If You Think You Have a Problem

If you are engaged in a relationship you think is problematic or have been following billing practices you now realize were wrong:

- Immediately cease filing the problematic bills.
- Seek knowledgeable legal counsel.
- Determine what money you collected in error from your patients and from the Federal health care programs and report and return overpayments.
- Unwind the problematic investment.
- Disentangle yourself from the suspicious relationship.
- Consider using OIG's or CMS's self-disclosure protocols.

OIG Provider Self-Disclosure Protocol

The OIG Provider Self-Disclosure Protocol is a vehicle for physicians to voluntarily disclose self-discovered evidence of potential fraud. The protocol allows providers to work with the Government to avoid the costs and disruptions entailed in a Government-directed investigation. For more information on the OIG Provider Self-Disclosure Protocol, see http://oig.hhs.gov/fraud/selfdisclosure.asp.

Case Examples of Physician Liabilities Resolved Under the OIG Provider Self-Disclosure Protocol

CASE EXAMPLES

- A Minneapolis physician paid $53,400 and resolved liability for violating his Medicare assignment agreement by charging patients a yearly fee for services, some of which were covered by Medicare.
- A Florida physician paid $100,000 and resolved liability related to referring patients to a lab owned by his brother.
- A neurosurgery practice paid $10,000 and resolved liability for employing an individual who was excluded from participation in the Federal health care programs.

What To Do If You Have Information About Fraud and Abuse Against Federal Health Care Programs

If you have information about fraud and abuse against Federal health care programs, use the OIG Fraud Hotline to report that information to the appropriate authorities. The Hotline allows the option of reporting anonymously.

Phone:	1-800-HHS-TIPS (1-800-447-8477)
Fax:	1-800-223-8164
Email:	HHSTIPS@oig.hhs.gov
TTY:	1-800-377-4950
Mail:	Office of Inspector General Department of Health & Human Services Attn: HOTLINE P.O. Box 23489 Washington, DC 20026

For additional information about the Hotline, visit the OIG Web site at http://oig.hhs.gov/fraud/hotline/.

CHAPTER 6
THE BIGGEST MISTAKES DOCTORS MAKE

The foregoing pages of this book are designed to show you how to protect you your family and your medical practice. Now we can talk about the biggest mistakes that doctors make, and how to avoid them so that you have assets to protect. You can read on to see what mistakes you may have already made, and what mistakes you can avoid making going forwards.

THE BIGGEST MISTAKES DOCTORS MAKE:

1. Failure to Maintain and Appropriately Use Independent Professional Advisors. We already discussed finding an appropriately qualified lawyer for your asset protection and estate planning, but your arsenal of advisors should extend beyond your lawyer. Many of the calamities described below will be avoided if a medical practice has experienced advisors on board. The practice should consult with its advisors when making major practice decisions, and also periodically confirm that appropriate procedures and safeguards are in place.

   (a) CPA: Quite often the quarterback of the advisor team will be a good, caring Certified Public Accountant who does extensive medical practice work. CPAs are often well versed in investments, business matters, and methods of financially theft-proofing a medical practice.

   CPAs should prepare quarterly or monthly financial statements for the medical practice; these statements should involve a review of accounts receivable, cash flow and general practice financial information.

   (b) Attorney: An experienced lawyer who represents a number of medical practices should have sufficient experience to help physicians avoid terrible problems before they occur.

   Just as physicians advise patients to have an annual check-up, a medical practice client should confer with his or her lawyer on a periodic basis. Commonly the primary lawyer for the practice will refer matters to appropriate sub-specialist attorneys in a number of different areas. Often this happens in conjunction with a CPA meeting.

   (c) Other Advisors: Other advisors commonly and appropriately used by a medical practice group will include (i) a qualified pension plan advisor, who is also preferably an actuary, as well as (ii) a banker who is knowledgeable as to practical business expense and loan-associated planning, and (iii) a reputable and conservative financial advisor or advisors who assist with pension planning, various insurances, and other practice-associated financial instruments.

Good advisors should be honest and always let the physician and the rest of the team know about questions, concerns, or the need to bring in additional experts to handle any particular matter or situation. Advisors who show up to sell only a single product or scheme often cause problems.

2. Failure to Maintain Medical Law Compliance. A great many physicians are annihilated financially when Medicare and/or private insurance carriers request hundreds of thousands of dollars in refunds because the physician has used inappropriate billing practices or financial arrangements with third parties. In many cases, these problems are reported to the government by employees who can earn a 15% "whistle-blower fee."

   Many physician clients simply do not realize they are using improper coding, do not maintain sufficient patient file back-up, or bill for items that are inappropriately unbundled or altogether un-billable.

   Reasonable and periodic practice maintenance and review by trusted medical consultant advisors eliminates the need for a more costly venture, such as a medical practice audit. In the author's experience, most medical practices benefit from hiring an independent consultant to come into the practice, perhaps annually, to spend a day randomly reviewing patient charts and the billing and collection processes associated therewith.

   Quite often, a good consultant can spot billing opportunities where the practice is under-charging or not charging at all for certain services. An independent consultant can also be a tactful go-between in conveying to some medical practice members that their file documentation is not sufficient. Such corrections are best conveyed by a neutral third party.

   Consultants should be hired by a lawyer on behalf of the medical practices, so that any problems discovered can stay confidential under the attorney-client privilege to the extent possible.

   If and when the government criticizes a medical practice's coding, file documentation or other billing procedures, it is very helpful to be able to show that the practice conscientiously hired and followed the advice of a reputable billing and coding consultant on a periodic basis.

   Many physician groups are also unfamiliar with or intentionally disregard rules relating to arm's-length leases, compensation arrangements, and referrals or testing within a group medical practice. The author has had law-abiding and well-meaning physician clients arrested in their lobbies by the FBI as a result of being in business with the wrong people at the wrong time.

Doctors can rest assured that any "scoundrel" that they have legitimate or questionable business relationships with will turn them in to get amnesty if and when approached by law enforcement, even if the doctor did nothing wrong. When law enforcement comes knocking the doctor should immediately have appropriate sub-specialty lawyers contact law enforcement on his or her behalf. Neither the doctor nor his or her staff should directly speak with any law enforcement officers at any time on any topic.

3. Failure to Maintain Proper Malpractice Insurance. While malpractice insurance is not inexpensive, it is necessary in order to protect physicians from the significant legal fees, expert witness costs, and liability exposure associated with defending lawsuits. The proliferation of the personal injury lawyer industry shows no sign of slowing down, and a sympathetic jury system, coupled with experts willing to testify that a doctor committed malpractice under complicated circumstances that a jury can never understand provides good cause for maintaining appropriate malpractice insurance coverage.

   Many advisors and clients believe that a practice need only maintain the lowest limits of liability coverage because "they will always settle for your limits," but we have already discussed the essential rashness and untruth of such a statement in earlier sections. The authors advise physician clients to have higher levels of liability insurance than the legally required minimum.

   Many physicians will obtain malpractice insurance coverage from low-cost carriers that turn out to be infirm and go bankrupt, leaving doctors high and dry to defend their own claims and without any coverage whatsoever for legal and expert expenses. Therefore, any opportunity to pay significantly less than the going rate for malpractice coverage should be reviewed carefully.

   Also, the income tax laws permit a medical group to form its own "captive insurance carrier" and deduct premiums paid to the carrier company. Under the tax law, the carrier company may not have to include premiums received as income unless or until it is determined what portion of the premiums will be used to pay claims as expenses and what portion of the premiums will be profits. Profits taken out later may be taxed at favorable capital gains rates.

   Nevertheless, this is a significant economic risk, since the carrier could "go under" if there are extensive claims, and when there are multiple doctors being insured by the carrier, one or two doctors who make a lot of mistakes could cost all of the equity for the other doctors.

   Further, unlike conventional malpractice insurance, which requires a carrier to offer tail malpractice insurance coverage at the request of each doctor, captive insurance carrier reinsurance contracts may not bind the reinsurance company to renew the coverage, let alone provide a tail policy on termination, leaving an entire group of doctors without any coverage whatsoever. Successor carriers will not provide tail coverage for periods of time when no other carrier is on the hook.

We have also discussed the dangers of "going bare", which can occur when a doctor has malpractice insurance provided by a carrier who is not state-registered. A possible loss of license can occur if a doctor cannot satisfy a claim by reason of not having malpractice insurance or the financial wherewithal to pay a claim.

Many doctors are not aware that for a small additional premium, they can have a separate "corporate" malpractice insurance policy issued by the same carrier that provides individual policies that covers the medical practice company. This effectively doubles the limits of malpractice insurance that would be available to pay on a claim, and assures that the company will have coverage if one of the doctors leaves and refuses to buy tail malpractice insurance.

Furthermore, nurse practitioners and registered nurses can often qualify for insurance with high limits of liability for very low cost. Many physicians will not treat certain types of high-risk patients unless they at all times have a nurse practitioner in the room with them to make sure that there is plenty of coverage, witnesses to what is said, and appropriate follow-up.

4. Failure of Multiple Physician-Owned Practices to Have Appropriate Buy/Sell and/or Shareholder Agreements in Place. Many successful medical practices are run on a handshake or a long-forgotten and now archaic agreement, but when problems or changes in circumstances arise the results can be catastrophic for the physicians - though quite lucrative for the legal profession.

   Example: Doctor A and Doctor B are lifelong friends who have practiced together 25 years and share 50% each ownership of a medical practice without current legal agreements. Their spouses have also been best friends.

   They have always worked approximately the same and have always been paid the same. A couple of years ago they were offered $3,000,000 for the practice, which involved signing 5 year non-competes and 5-year employment agreements. They also own the practice real estate together in a separate company under which they have signed a $2,000,000 mortgage on real estate now worth only $1,500,000.

   If Doctor A becomes disabled, they may not be able to agree on how much Doctor B should be paid to administer the practice. Disagreements may also arise regarding the hiring of a replacement doctor or doctors.

They may also not be able to agree on a price or terms for Doctor B to buy Doctor A out.

Often disabled or injured physicians believe they may be able to return to work. Meanwhile, their partners take a more cautious view of their capacity for recovery. The practice can be significantly damaged during this period of time until the disabled physician's status on returning to work is absolutely confirmed.

What if Doctor A is faced with drug addiction or begins having an affair with medical practice personnel that could cause obliteration of the practice? How can Doctor B force Doctor A to leave, or to even behave? How can Doctor B protect the practice and himself from responsibility for Doctor A's difficulties?

What if Doctor A dies? Doctor A's widow may believe that the practice is worth $3,000,000 and will be voting Doctor A's stock unless or until she is bought out. How can Doctor B convince Doctor A's widow and her lawyers and valuation experts that the practice has lost significant value because of Doctor A's death? How can Doctor B run the practice, if Doctor A's widow will not agree to any significant changes in situations where such changes become necessary?

How can Doctor B attract a new doctor to the practice if he has to disclose that he is not getting along with the 50% widow owner of the practice?

The list of examples goes on and on. It does take time and money to put together an appropriate Buy-Sell/Employment/Shareholder document package. Almost no two are the same as circumstances change. However, it is a valuable investment that every practice should make.

In addition, applicable state law and/or Medicare law often requires that compensation be based upon methods determined in advance that do not take into account the referral of patient services. As mentioned under number 2 above, the referral of a patient within a group practice for certain testing or other "designated health services" under the Stark Law can be a felony unless there is a properly documented method of sharing that qualifies under the Stark Laws. Failure to have this in writing in advance of a particular calendar quarter can constitute a felony offense.

5. Failure to Procure and Maintain Proper Insurances. There are myriad insurances required to appropriately safeguard a medical practices from the normal risks of doing business, particularly in view of the American trial system.

   Fortunately most of these risks can be reasonably handled on an affordable basis, assuming that proper coverage is in place.

The most important coverage is clearly malpractice insurance, which we have already addressed, and which is mentioned below as a separate section, but other insurances which are essential to the well-being of physicians and their medical practices include:

(a) Disability insurance;

(b) Overhead insurance to handle practice expenses during a period of disability or in the event of a natural disaster such as a hurricane or acts of terrorism;

(c) Liability insurance to cover non-malpractice obligations, such as if patients or others hurt themselves in the parking lot or fall on slippery areas in the office;

(d) Workers' compensation insurance to protect the practice against state laws that can require lifetime support and/or significant monetary payments to be made to an employee injured in the course of employment; and

(e) Unowned automobile liability insurance to insure against the liability that occurs to a medical practice if any employee is in an automobile accident while running errands or otherwise working in the course of medical practice business.

We have also discussed the risks of inadequate automobile liability coverage; the authors typically recommend at least $3,000,000 - $5,000,000 worth of umbrella liability coverage to cover all business and personal driving, and driving by others who might use the doctor's car.

There are thousands of disabled physicians in the United States now living on disability insurance. The author has more than 15 clients who have been able to "retire" on their disability insurance. This explains why the rates are so high to procure such coverage, but also why having good coverage is a necessity rather than a luxury for physicians who do not have adequate retirement savings to support themselves and their families for their remaining lifetimes.

Sometimes individual health insurance policies will not cover on-the-job injuries, under the presumption that a doctor will be covered under workers' compensation for on-the-job injuries. Doctors who do not have workers' compensation insurance, which is often waived to save money, should check their health insurance policies to make sure that they are covered for on-the-job injuries.

6. Failure to Make the Medical Practice and the Doctor Judgment-Proof. We have extensively discussed how to protect a medical practice and its assets; failure to do so can be devastating to a doctor and his or her family. There are many ways that a medical practice and a doctor can work to make themselves a less attractive target for a plaintiff's lawyer.

Often the practice incurs debt in its name, and the lender or lenders have liens on practice and personal assets that must be paid before a plaintiff is able to levy upon a doctor or practice. Also, valuable assets like real estate and furniture and equipment can be owned by a separate entity that would lease those assets to the medical practice to make them inaccessible, or at least less accessible, to a malpractice claimant.

It is also important to ensure that each physician in a group has his or her personal creditor protection planning properly in place so that a plaintiff lawyer can be led to settle within policy limits if and when a catastrophic lawsuit occurs.

Because of state and bankruptcy law fraudulent transfer law statutes, it is often crucial that creditor protection planning for the medical practice entity and the doctors occur well before any problems arise.

When a serious lawsuit occurs, the doctors should keep in mind that the lawyer hired by the insurance company does not necessarily have duty of absolute loyalty to the doctor. The malpractice insurance carrier selects and pays the lawyer.

There are often circumstances whereby an independent lawyer should be hired by the doctor to encourage the insurance carrier to settle a claim within policy limits when the opportunity arises, in order not to risk the doctor's personal and practice assets to an "excess verdict." We have also discussed the "bad faith" rules, under which many states have laws that will require an insurance carrier to be responsible for any excess verdict, if proper demand has been made upon the carrier when it had the opportunity to settle within policy limits.

7. Failure to Theft-Proof the Practice's Monies and Accounts Receivable. The author regularly receives at least one phone call per year from a very upset physician who has had tens of thousands of practice dollars stolen by an employee. This employee has often been with the practice many years, and most of the time is the most trusted person in the practice other than the physicians themselves. As such, the employee is able to obtain physical possession of checks made payable to the practice by one or more payor sources and/or has written checks on the practice accounts for bogus expenses.

   Over the years, we have seen medical practices unwillingly and unwittingly pay credit card expenses, electric company expenses, car payments, and even home mortgage payments for a medical practice employee. When the circumstances are reviewed, they reveal that most of these situations would have been avoidable with proper supervision and use of appropriate safeguards.

   Additionally, money is often stolen from practice accounts when large projects such as buildings, construction, or similar matters are administered by a person who signs the checks and/or administers the checks and invoices for a busy physician.

Most of the time the theft is carried out by a trusted office manager, without any assistance from another employee.

It is a very basic accounting system principle that the person or people who physically open the envelopes containing checks payable to the practice record the checks onto a log and ensure that the checks are properly deposited. These deposits are then reported to a separate employee who has the ability to record the payments in the practice's computer system.

It is a fatal error to allow one individual to have physical possession of checks and also the ability to enter payments or write-offs onto the practice's billing computer system. Even spouses have been known to steal from medical practices, especially when the practice has multiple partners.

Many practices use a post office box for checks to eliminate the risk of someone being able to "snatch a few checks from the mail" before they can be posted. Many banks offer check-depositing services and addresses that can be used as well. These are often known as "lock box" arrangements.

Larger practices can have someone from their CPA firm visit the practice on an annual basis without advance notice to the practice personnel. This demonstrates to employees that there is some degree of monitoring, and can discourage practice theft.

8. Using Greedy Investment Advisors. The number of different investments and life insurance and annuity arrangements that can be sold to doctors and their practices in the financial world is limitless, and growing! The quality of each particular investment vehicle can vary dramatically in terms of actual financial safety, conservative versus aggressive orientation, likelihood of being acceptable to the IRS in the event of an audit, and the amount of commission paid to advisors who may suggest such arrangements.

   Expecting a physician to read a prospectus or to understand a complicated tax maneuver is like expecting a lawyer or a CPA to read an EKG- it is easy to be mistaken!

   If the advisors are earning a significant portion of the amounts invested as compensation, a degree of manipulation, non-disclosure, exaggeration or outright lying can take place.

   In the pension world, actuaries and many CPA firms who practice extensively in the retirement plan arena can yield great results for clients. Pension and profit-sharing plans are well-protected under applicable creditor laws and well-accepted under the tax law in conventional form.

   More aggressive plans, such as 419A Welfare Benefit plans and 412i plans, should be examined carefully by independent advisors before investing.

The author urges clients to use independent accountants who are not compensated directly or indirectly for the sale of financial products. The author has seen entire fortunes lost to tax shelter deals in the 1970s, leveraged real estate deals in the 1980s, land development deals in the 1990s, and now Madoff and related Ponzi and margined-securities deals in recent years. Crime often pays, and the victim is the doctor who gets involved in these types of arrangements.

There is rarely a good reason for a pension or profit-sharing plan to own a life insurance or annuity product, except to compensate anyone who may be licensed in life insurance and annuities who has involvement in the pension or profit-sharing

9. Unbalanced Investment Portfolios. Statistical studies show that a diversified portfolio of investments will generally out perform a non-diversified portfolio, with significantly less risk. Many successful clients own investment real estate, mutual funds allocated among the various classes of stock investments, and bond funds or CDs. It almost never makes sense for anyone to put all of their eggs in one basket.

   Go for singles and doubles instead of home runs. Time and time again we have seen physicians place significant portions of their financial assets into high risk investments or ventures with the intention of hitting "a home run" under risky circumstances. In our experience, these clients almost always strike out. Many end up working full time into their 70s, and eventually retire only by selling their home and living in an apartment.

   There is almost always a direct and opposite correlation between expected rate of return and risk being taken. Many high income professionals recognize this and are nevertheless willing to take risks. Quite often, however, physician investors are assured that an arrangement is "virtually risk free" even though it is expected (or touted) to yield a significant return. If it seems too good to be true, it probably is.

10. Doing Business with the Wrong People. Unfortunately, crime, and also deceitful or misleading behavior can be lucrative for the "bad apple", and these individuals are often found courting doctors to do business and investment transactions or to provide consulting services.

   Since the overwhelming majority of doctors are very honest and do not have formal business training, it is not difficult to market "unique propositions" to doctors and to eventually find a handful of doctors who may succumb to participate in a recommended arrangement.

   Commonly these "bad apples" will present themselves through relatives, friends and possibly even misled advisors.

   Typically the doctor will be asked to invest in a startup or growing company, to help start a new business, or to be involved in the purchasing or financing of real estate.

Bad apples are often well-dressed, exhibit success in the forms of nice house and cars, and sometimes even jet airplanes, stunning vacations, trophy wives, and impressive club memberships.

A team of advisors can usually sniff out this type of individual or organization by checking references, or the lack thereof, licensing, and with other professionals who have worked with the applicable individual. The author has seen these characters in billing companies, unique invention startups, real estate ventures, medical related companies, ice machines (that did not exist), Ponzi schemes, and other situations.

Do not forget the adage about the experienced businessman and the doctor who become partners. The businessman puts in his experience and the doctor puts in his money. At the end of the day the businessman has the money and the doctor merely has an experience!

Doctors with gambling addiction tendencies are often drawn to elusive schemes where the doctor is told that he or she has earned millions of dollars and should have colleagues put money in so that they can earn millions too, while in reality the "con job" is that the money is being stolen or used to pay debts on assets that will never be worth anything. A junior Madoff may be your next door neighbor or brother-in-law!

Every year the IRS publishes the "Dirty Dozen," a list of tax frauds, including schemes involving the internet, domestic tax crimes, offshore frauds and false claims for refunds. This is done for the benefit of citizens and their awareness of financial predators. The IRS website at http://www.irs.gov/newsroom/article/0,id=206370,00.html says it right: "Taxpayers should be wary of scams to avoid paying taxes that seem too good to be true, especially during these challenging economic times," Commissioner Doug Shulman said. "There is no secret trick that can eliminate a person's tax obligations. People should be wary of anyone peddling any of these scams."

11. Failure to Have Anyone in the Practice Pay Attention to Contracts with Third Parties. Quite often medical practices get into disputes or find themselves stuck in agreements as a result of a trusting nature or lack of attention to details associated with contracts they enter into with third parties. Say, for example, somebody delivers a copier to the medical practice that the office manager has requested on a trial basis. Upon delivery, that person gets the receptionist to sign a contract accepting copier and binding the practice to 48 months of payments.

    Another example is when a medical practice has a lease that gives the doctors the right to extend after a certain date, but they forget to give notice of extension by the deadline. The practice gets held up by the landlord for a larger rent payment or has to vacate and find new property.

A third example is when a lease for a large piece of equipment also requires the practice to maintain the equipment with one company only. The company may provide poor service or may not permit the practice to pre-pay the lease or re-finance it from a high rate of interest without paying tens of thousands of dollars in penalties.

Another trap some practices fall into is using an office manager or non-CPA accountant to draft legal documents that employ physicians, or to set up companies for the practice, not realizing that the contracts have inappropriate provisions or do not cover essential items that a lawyer or appropriately qualified advisor would have pointed out.

F. Lee Bailey, a famous criminal defense lawyer, said that "anyone who acts as his own lawyer has a fool for a client." Most successful lawyers hire other lawyers to do work for them personally when it is outside of their area of specialty, or sometimes even when it is within their area of specialty because of this phenomenon.

An article written by the author on Mistakes Doctors Make Managing Thri Practices and Investments is as follows:

MISTAKES DOCTORS MAKE MANAGING THEIR PRACTICES AND INVESTMENTS

By: Alan S. Gassman

Reprinted with permission from Leimberg Information Services - Steve Leimberg's Estate Planning Newsletter - Archive Message #1465 20-May-09

EXECUTIVE SUMMARY:

This commentary reviews ten avoidable mistakes that can be the cause of fatal errors for medical practices and investment portfolios.

COMMENT:

While different physicians and groups of physicians tend to make more mistakes in one area than another, each common mistake area should be reviewed and understood with appropriate advisors. These common errors, which are described in more detail below, are as follows (hyperlinked for your convenience):

1. Failure to Maintain and Appropriately Use Independent Professional Advisors.
2. Failure to Maintain Medical Law Compliance.
3. Failure to Maintain Proper Malpractice Insurance.
4. Failure of Multiple Physician-Owned Practices to Have Appropriate Buy-Sell and/ or Shareholder Agreements in Place.
5. Failure to Procure and Maintain Proper Insurances.
6. Failure to Make the Medical Practice and Doctor Judgment-Proof.

MISTAKES DOCTORS MAKE MANAGING THEIR PRACTICES AND INVESTMENTS
By: Alan S. Gassman

7. Failure to Theft-Proof the Practice's Monies and Accounts Receivable.
8. Using Greedy Investment Advisors.
9. Doing Business With the Wrong People.
10. Failure to Have Anyone in the Practice Pay Attention to Contracts with Third Parties.

1. Failure to Maintain and Appropriately Use Independent Professional Advisors.

Many of the calamities described below will be avoided if a medical practice has experienced advisors on board. The practice should consult with its advisors when making major practice decisions, and also periodically confirm that appropriate procedures and safeguards are in place.

(1) CPA: Quite often the quarterback of the advisor team will be a good, caring Certified Public Accountant who does extensive medical practice work. CPA's are often well versed in investments, business matters, and methods of theft- proofing a medical practice from a financial standpoint.

CPAs should prepare quarterly or monthly financial statements for the medical practice; these statements should involve a review of accounts receivable, cash flow and general practice financial information.

(2) Attorney: An experienced lawyer who represents a number of medical practices should have sufficient experience to help physicians avoid terrible problems before they occur.

Just as physicians advise patients to have an annual check-up, and may wisely require this before prescriptions are renewed beyond 12 months, a medical practice client should confer with its lawyer on a periodic basis. Commonly the primary lawyer for the practice will refer matters to appropriate sub-specialist attorneys in a number of different areas. Often this happens in conjunction with a CPA meeting.

(3) Other Advisors: Other advisors commonly and appropriately used by a medical practice group will include (i) a qualified pension plan advisor, who is also preferably an actuary, as well as (ii) a banker who is knowledgeable as to practical business expense and loan-associated planning, and (iii) a reputable and conservative financial advisor or advisors who assist with pension planning, various insurances, and other practice-associated financial instruments.

Good advisors should be honest and always let the physician and the rest of the team know about questions, concerns, or the need to bring in additional experts to handle any particular matter or situation. Advisors who show up to sell a single product or scheme commonly cause problems, as described in below.

2. Failure to Maintain Medical Law Compliance.

A great many physicians are annihilated financially when Medicare and/or private insurance carriers request hundreds of thousands of dollars in refunds because the physician has used inappropriate billing practices or financial arrangements with third parties. In many cases these problems are reported to the government by employees who can earn a 15% "whistle-blower fee."

Many physician clients simply do not realize that they use improper coding, do not maintain sufficient patient file back-up, or bill for items that are inappropriately unbundled or altogether un-billable.

Several years ago, the concept of a "medical practice compliance audit" was in vogue, and many professionals, in the opinion of the author, significantly over-charged physician groups for "practice audits." Such audits extended far beyond a reasonable review of billing, patient file documentation, and third-party financial arrangement review.

Reasonable and periodic practice maintenance and reviewed by trusted medical consultant advisors eliminates the need for such a costly venture. In the author's experience, most medical practices benefit from hiring an independent consultant to come into the practice, perhaps annually, to spend a day randomly reviewing patient charts and the billing and collection processes associated therewith.

Quite often a good consultant can spot billing opportunities where the practice is undercharging or not knowing to charge for certain services. An independent consultant can also be a tactful go-between to let certain members of a medical practice know that their file documentation is not sufficient. Such corrections are best conveyed by a neutral third party.

Consultants should be hired by a lawyer on behalf of the medical practice so that any problems they may discover can stay confidential under the attorney-client privilege to the extent possible.

MISTAKES DOCTORS MAKE MANAGING THEIR PRACTICES AND INVESTMENTS
By: Alan S. Gassman

If and when the government criticizes a medical practice's coding, file documentation or other billing procedures, it is very helpful to be able to show that the practice conscientiously hired and followed the advice of a reputable billing and coding consultant on a periodic basis.

Many physician groups are also unfamiliar with or intentionally disregard rules relating to arms length leases, compensation arrangements, and also the ability to refer tests within a group medical practice only if certain rules are followed. The author has had law-abiding and well-meaning physician clients arrested in their lobbies by the FBI as a result of being in business with the wrong people at the wrong time.

Doctors can rest assured that any "scoundrel" that they have legitimate or questionable business relationships with will turn them in to get amnesty if and when approached by law enforcement, even if the doctor did nothing wrong. When law enforcement comes knocking the doctor should immediately have appropriate sub-specialty lawyers contact law enforcement on his or her behalf. Neither the doctor nor his or her staff should directly speak with any law enforcement officers at any time on any topic.

3. Failure to Maintain Proper Malpractice Insurance.

While malpractice insurance is not inexpensive, it is necessary in order to protect physicians from the significant legal fees, expert witness costs, and liability exposure associated with defending lawsuits. The proliferation of the personal injury lawyer industry shows no sign of slowing down, and a sympathetic jury system, coupled with experts willing to testify that a doctor committed malpractice under complicated circumstances that a jury can never understand provides good cause for maintaining appropriate malpractice insurance coverage.

Many advisors and clients believe that a practice need only maintain the lowest limits of liability coverage because "they will always settle for your limits," but the author has found that in many cases plaintiffs will not settle for low limits of medical malpractice insurance liability where there are other significant assets exposed. Physician clients will sleep better and have a greater sense of financial security, as well as significantly less personal exposure, when they have higher levels of liability insurance than the legally required minimum.

Many physicians will obtain malpractice insurance coverage from low-cost carriers that turn out to be infirm and go bankrupt, leaving doctors high and dry to defend their own claims and without any coverage whatsoever for legal and expert expenses.

Any opportunity to pay significantly less than the going rate for malpractice coverage should be reviewed carefully with the above concerns in mind.

Also, the income tax laws permit a medical group to form its own "captive insurance carrier" and deduct premiums paid to the carrier company. Under the tax law the carrier company may not have to include premiums received as income unless or until it is determined what portion of the premiums will be used to pay claims as expenses and what portion of the premiums will be profits. Profits taken out later may be taxed at favorable capital gains rates.

Nevertheless, there is a significant economic risk taken since the carrier could "go under" if there are extensive claims, and when there are multiple doctors being insured by the carrier, one or two doctors who make a lot of mistakes could cost all of the equity for the other doctors.

Further, unlike conventional malpractice insurance, which requires a carrier to offer tail malpractice insurance coverage at the request of each doctor, captive insurance carrier reinsurance contracts will commonly not bind the reinsurance company to even renew the coverage, let alone provide a tail policy on termination, leaving an entire group of doctors without any coverage whatsoever. Successor carriers will not provide tail coverage for periods of time that no other carrier is on the hook for.

The laws of most states require that malpractice insurance be provided by a state-registered carrier. Doctors who have malpractice insurance furnished by an unregistered carrier may be considered to be "going bare" under state law, and may therefore have to notify patients that the doctor is "bare." A possible loss of license can occur if a doctor cannot satisfy a claim by reason of not having malpractice insurance or the financial wherewithal to pay a claim.

Many doctors are not aware that for a small additional premium they can have a separate "corporate" malpractice insurance policy issued by the same carrier that provides individual policies that covers the medical practice company in order to effectively double the limits of malpractice insurance that would be available to pay on a claim, and to assure that the company will have coverage if one of the doctors leaves and refuses to buy tail malpractice insurance.

Also, nurse practitioners and registered nurses can often qualify for insurance with high limits of liability for very low cost. Many physicians will not treat certain types of high-risk patients unless they at all times have a nurse practitioner in the room with them to make sure that there is plenty of coverage, witnesses to what is said, and appropriate follow-up.

4. Failure of Multiple Physician-Owned Practices to Have Appropriate Buy-Sell and/or Shareholder Agreements in Place.

Many successful medical practices are run on a handshake or a long-forgotten and now archaic agreement, but when problems or changes in circumstances arise the results can be catastrophic- and quite lucrative for the legal profession.

For the sake of example, assume that Doctor A and Doctor B are lifelong friends who have practiced together 25 years and share 50% each ownership of a medical practice without current legal agreements. Their spouses have also been best friends.

They have always worked approximately the same and have always been paid the same. A couple of years ago they were offered $3,000,000 for the practice, which involved signing 5 year non-competes and 5-year employment agreements. They also own the practice real estate together in a separate company under which they have signed a $2,000,000 mortgage on real estate now worth only $1,500,000.

If Doctor A becomes disabled, they may not be able to agree on how much Doctor B should be paid to administer the practice. Disagreements may also arise regarding the hiring of a replacement doctor or doctors.

They may also not be able to agree on a price or terms for Doctor B to buy Doctor A out.

Often disabled physicians believe they will be returning to work. Meanwhile, their partners see the writing on the wall and take a more skeptical view of their capacity for recovery. The practice can be significantly damaged during this period of time until the disabled physician's status on returning to work is absolutely confirmed.

What if Doctor A becomes a drug addict or begins having an affair with medical practice personnel that could cause obliteration of the practice? How can Doctor B force Doctor A to leave, or to even behave? How can Doctor B protect the practice and himself from responsibility for Doctor A's misconduct?

What if Doctor A dies? Doctor A's widow may believe that the practice is worth $3,000,000 and will be voting Doctor A's stock unless or until she is bought out. How can Doctor B convince Doctor A and her lawyers and valuation experts that the practice has lost significant value because of Doctor A's death? How can Doctor B run the practice if Doctor A's widow will not agree to any significant changes in situations where such changes become necessary?

How can Doctor B attract a new doctor to the practice if he has to disclose that he is not getting along with the 50% widow owner of the practice?

The list of examples goes on and on. It does take time and money to put together an appropriate Buy-Sell/Employment/Shareholder document package. Almost no two are the same as circumstances change. However, it is a valuable investment that every practice should make.

In addition, applicable state law and/or Medicare law often requires that compensation be based upon methods determined in advance that do not take into account the referral of patient services. As mentioned under number 2 above, the referral of a patient within a group practice for certain testing or other "designated health services" under the Stark Law can be a felony unless there is a properly documented method of sharing that qualifies under the Stark Laws. Failure to have this in writing in advance of a particular calendar quarter can constitute a felony offense.

5. Failure to Procure and Maintain Proper Insurances.

There are myriad insurances required to appropriately safeguard a medical practices from the normal risks of doing business, particularly in view of the American trial system.

Fortunately most of these risks can be reasonably handled on an affordable basis, assuming that proper coverage is in place.

The most important coverage is clearly malpractice insurance, which is addressed below as a separate section, but other insurances which are essential to the well-being of physicians and their medical practices include:

1) disability insurance,

2) overhead insurance to handle practice expenses during a period of disability or in the event of a natural disaster such as a hurricane or acts of terrorism,

3) liability insurance to cover non-malpractice obligations, such as if patients or others hurt themselves in the parking lot or fall on slippery areas in the office,

4) workers' compensation insurance to protect the practice against state laws that can require lifetime support and/or significant monetary payments to be made to an employee injured in the course of employment, and

5) unowned automobile liability insurance to insure against the liability that occurs to a medical practice if any employee is in an automobile accident while running errands or otherwise working in the course of medical practice business.

Individual automobile liability policies should also be reviewed to ensure that each physician has coverage for medical practice-related driving. Many personal policies will not cover business driving without additional policy riders. The author commonly recommends at least $3,000,000 - $5,000,000 worth of umbrella liability coverage to cover all business and personal driving, and driving by others who might use the doctor's car.

There are thousands of disabled physicians in the United States now living on disability insurance. The author has more than 15 clients who have been able to "retire" on their disability insurance. This explains why the rates are so high to procure such coverage, but also why having good coverage is a necessity rather than a luxury for physicians who do not have adequate retirement savings to support themselves and their families for their remaining lifetimes.

Sometimes individual health insurance policies will not cover on-the-job injuries under the presumption that a doctor will be covered under workers' compensation for on-the-job injuries. Doctors who do not have workers' compensation insurance, which is often waived to save money, should check their health insurance policies to make sure that they are covered for on-the-job injuries.

6. Failure to Make the Medical Malpractice and Doctor Judgment-Proof.

There are many ways that a medical practice and a doctor can work to make themselves a less attractive target for a plaintiff's lawyer.

Often the practice incurs debt in its name, and the lender or lenders have liens on practice and personal assets that must be paid before a plaintiff is able to levy upon a doctor or practice. Also, valuable assets like real estate and furniture and equipment can be owned by a separate entity that would lease those assets to the medical practice to make them inaccessible, or at least less accessible, to a malpractice claimant.

It is also important to ensure that each physician in a group has his or her personal creditor protection planning properly in place so that a plaintiff lawyer can be led to settle within policy limits if and when a catastrophic lawsuit occurs.

Because of state and bankruptcy law fraudulent transfer law statutes, it is often crucial that creditor protection planning for the medical practice entity and the doctors occur well before any problems arise.

When a serious lawsuit occurs, the doctors should keep in mind that the lawyer hired by the insurance company does not necessarily have duty of absolute loyalty to the doctor. The malpractice insurance carrier selects and pays the lawyer.

There are often circumstances whereby an independent lawyer should be hired by the doctor to encourage the insurance carrier to settle a claim within policy limits when the opportunity arises, in order not to risk the doctor's personal and practice assets to an "excess verdict." Many states have laws that will require an insurance carrier to be responsible for any excess verdict if proper demand has been made upon the carrier when it had the opportunity to settle within policy limits. These are called the "bad faith" rules.

7. Failure to Theft-Proof the Practice's Monies and Accounts Receivable.

The author regularly receives at least one phone call per year from a very upset physician who has had tens of thousands of practice dollars stolen by an employee. This employee has often been with the practice many years, and most of the time is the most trusted person in the practice other than the physicians themselves. As such, the employee is able to obtain physical possession of checks made payable to the practice by one or more payor sources and/or has written checks on the practice accounts for bogus expenses.

Over the years, the author has seen medical practices unwillingly and unwittingly pay credit card expenses, electric company expenses, car payments, and even home mortgage payments for a medical practice employee. When the circumstances are reviewed, they reveal that most of these situations would have been avoidable with proper supervision and use of appropriate safeguards.

Additionally, money is often stolen from practice accounts when large projects such as buildings, construction, or similar matters are administered by a person who signs the checks and/or administers the checks and invoices for a busy physician.

Most of the time the theft is carried out by the most trusted office manager without any assistance from another employee.

It is a very basic accounting system principle that the person or people who physically open the envelopes containing checks payable to the practice record the checks onto a log and ensure that the checks are properly deposited. These deposits are then reported to a separate employee who has the ability to record the payments in the practice's computer system.

It is a fatal error to allow one individual to have physical possession of checks and also the ability enter payments or write-offs onto the practice's billing computer system. Even spouses have been known to steal from medical practices, especially when there are multiple partners.

Many practices use a post office box for checks to eliminate the risk of someone being able to "snatch a few checks from the mail" before they can be posted. Many banks offer check-depositing services and addresses that can be used as well. These are often known as "lock box" arrangements.

Larger practices can have someone from their CPA firm visit the practice on an annual basis without advance notice to the practice personnel. This demonstrates to employees that there is some degree of monitoring going on and can discourage practice theft.

8. Using Greedy Investment Advisors.

The number of different investments and life insurance and annuity arrangements that can be sold to doctors and their practices in the financial world. The quality of each particular investment vehicle can vary dramatically in terms of actual financial safety, conservative versus aggressive orientation, likelihood of being acceptable to the IRS in the event of an audit, and as to the amount of commissions paid to advisors who may suggest such arrangements.

MISTAKES DOCTORS MAKE MANAGING THEIR PRACTICES AND INVESTMENTS
By: Alan S. Gassman

Expecting a physician to read a prospectus or to understand a complicated tax maneuver is like expecting a lawyer or a CPA to read an EKG- it is easy to be fooled!

If the advisors are earning a significant portion of the amounts invested as compensation, a degree of manipulation, non-disclosure, exaggeration or outright lying can take place.

In the pension world, actuaries and many CPA firms who practice extensively in the retirement plan arena can yield the great results for clients. Pension and profit-sharing plans are well-protected under applicable creditor laws and well-accepted under the tax law in conventional form.

More aggressive plans such as 419A Welfare Benefit plans and 412i plans should be examined carefully by independent advisors before investing.

The author urges clients to use independent accountants who are not compensated directly or indirectly for the sale of financial products. The author has seen entire fortunes lost to tax shelter deals in the 1970s, leveraged real estate deals in the 1980s, land development deals in the 1990s, and now Madoff and related Ponzi and margined-securities deals in the present decade. Crime often pays, and the victim is the doctor who gets involved in these types of arrangements.

There is rarely a good reason for a pension or profit-sharing plan to own a life insurance or annuity product, except to compensate anyone who may be licensed in life insurance and annuities who has involvement in the pension or profit-sharing

9. Doing Business with the Wrong People.

Unfortunately, crime, and also deceitful or misleading behavior can be lucrative for the "bad or careless actor," and these individuals are often found courting doctors to do business and investment transactions or to provide consulting services.

Since the overwhelming majority of doctors are very honest and do not have formal business training, it is not difficult to market "unique propositions" to doctors and to eventually find a handful of doctors who may succumb to participate in a recommended arrangement.

Commonly these "bad actors" will present themselves through relatives, friends and possibly even misled advisors.

MISTAKES DOCTORS MAKE MANAGING THEIR PRACTICES AND INVESTMENTS

By: Alan S. Gassman

Typically the doctor will be asked to invest in a startup or growing company, to help start a new business, or to be involved in the purchasing or financing of real estate.

Bad actors are often well-dressed, exhibit success in the forms of nice house and cars, and sometimes even jet airplanes, stunning vacations, trophy wives, and impressive club memberships.

A team of advisors can usually sniff out this type of individual or organization by checking references, or the lack thereof, licensing, and with other professionals who have worked with the applicable individual. The author has seen this occur in billing companies, unique invention startups, real estate ventures, medical related companies, ice machines (that did not exist), Ponzi schemes, and other situations.

If it sounds too good to be true it usually is! And do not forget the adage about the experienced businessman and the doctor who become partners. The businessman puts in his experience and the doctor puts in his money. At the end of the day the businessman has the money and the doctor merely has an experience!

Doctors with gamble-holic tendencies are often drawn to elusive schemes where the doctor is told that he or she has earned millions of dollars and should have colleagues put money in so that they can earn millions too, while in reality the "con job" is that the money is being stolen or used to pay debts on assets that will never be worth anything. A junior Madoff may be your next door neighbor or brother-in-law!

Every year the IRS publishes the "Dirty Dozen," a list of tax frauds, including schemes involving the internet, domestic tax crimes, offshore frauds and false claims for refunds. This is done for the benefit of citizens and their awareness of financial predators. The IRS website at http://www.irs.gov/newsroom/article/0,id=206370,00.html says it right:

"Taxpayers should be wary of scams to avoid paying taxes that seem too good to be true, especially during these challenging economic times,"

Commissioner Doug Shulman said.

"There is no secret trick that can eliminate a person's tax obligations. People should be wary of anyone peddling any of these scams."

MISTAKES DOCTORS MAKE MANAGING THEIR PRACTICES AND INVESTMENTS

By: Alan S. Gassman

10. Failure to Have Anyone in the Practice Pay Attention to Contracts with Third Parties.

Quite often medical practices get into disputes or find themselves stuck in agreements as a result of a trusting nature or lack of attention to details associated with contracts they enter into with third parties. Say, for example, somebody delivers a copier to the medical practice that the office manager has requested on a trial basis. Upon delivery, that person gets the receptionist to sign a contract accepting copier and binding the practice to 48 months of payments.

Another example is when a medical practice has a lease that gives the doctors the right to extend after a certain date, but they forget to give notice of extension by the deadline. The practice gets held up by the landlord for a larger rent payment or has to vacate and find new property.

A third example is when a lease for a large piece of equipment also requires the practice to maintain the equipment with one company only. The company may provide poor service or may not permit the practice to pre-pay the lease or re-finance it from a high rate of interest without paying tens of thousands of dollars in penalties.

Another trap some practices fall into is using an office manager or non-CPA accountant to draft legal documents that employ physicians or to set up companies for the practice, not realizing that the contracts have inappropriate provisions or do not cover essential items that a lawyer or appropriately qualified advisor would have pointed out.

F. Lee Baily said that *"anyone who acts as his own lawyer has a fool for a client."*

Most successful lawyers hire other lawyers to do work for them personally when it is outside of their area of specialty, or sometimes even when it is within their area of specialty because of this phenomenon.

If lawyers are smart enough not to do legal work for themselves, why aren't doctors and their other advisors?

CHAPTER 7
LESTER PERLING'S HYPOTHETICALS

The following are hypotheticals posed by co-author Lester Perling in a webinar dated February 19, 2013 that can be viewed at www.gassmanlawassociates.com/webinars

HYPOTHETICAL #1

Your client is the administrator of a group practice. The practice has decided that because of the administrative burdern and costs associated with collections, it would just waive copayments and deductibles for its insured patients but continue to charge the insurer the usual and customary charge for the service. In addition, the practice is establishing a prompt payment discount for patients that fulfill their cost-sharing obligations at the time of service. This prompt payment discount would be applied contemporaneously to the services provided to the patient.

KICKBACK ISSUES

Federal Law - The federal Anti-kickback statute is a criminal statute that prohibits the exchange of anything of value, in an effort to induce (or reward) the referral of federal health care business (42 U.S.C. § 1320a-7b).

There is a safe harbor for waivers of beneficiary coinsurance and deductible amounts but it only applies to inpatient services (42 CFR § 1001.952(k)).

However, HHS-OIG opined in its 2008 advisory opinion that prompt payment discounts are generally allowable as long as the discount is not a means to induce patients to self-refer. Advisory Opinion 08-03 (Feb. 8, 2008), https://oig.hhs.gov/fraud/docs/advisoryopinions/2008/AdvOpn08-03A.pdf.

HYPOTHETICAL #2

Your client is a solo physician practice. A police officer comes to the practice and asks questions about the treatment provided to a particular patient. The police officer explains that he is conducting a preliminary investigation involving that patient and explains that he needs to know what medication the physician has prescribed to the patient. The police officer does not have a court order or subpoena for the medical records. How should you advise the physician to respond to the police officer's request?

FEDERAL LAW

HIPAA: The Privacy Rule permits health care providers to comply with court orders or court-ordered warrants, subpoenas or summons, grand jury subpoenas, and administrative summons or civil investigative demands. (45 CFR 164.512(f)(1)(ii)). Cannot turn over PHI if the police officer does not have the appropriate order.

In the case of an administrative summons or civil investigative demand, if de-identified information cannot reasonably be used, the information sought must be relevant and material to a legitimate law enforcement inquiry, and the request must be specific and limited in scope to the extent reasonably practicable in light of the purpose for which the information is sought.

DISCLOSURE OF SUBSTANCE ABUSE AND/OR MENTAL HEALTH RECORDS?

Federal Law - Under 42 U.S.C. § 290dd-2, records pertaining to substance abuse treatment are deemed confidential. These records can be disclosed if authorized by a court order. Court order must be issued if "good cause" is shown. Good cause means that disclosure is require to "avert a substantial risk of death or serious bodily harm." 42 U.S.C. § 290dd-2(b)(2)(B). Absent such court order, these records cannot be used to "initiate or substantiate" any criminal charges against a patient or to conduct an investigation of the patient.

Florida Law - Mental health records are confidential (Fla. Stat. § 394.4615). A specific court order is necessary for the release of this type of information. Similarly substance abuse records are also deemed confidential (Fla. Stat. § 397.501(7)) and can only be released to law enforcement personnel under very limited circumstances.

HYPOTHETICAL #3

You represent a physician practice that is enrolled in the Medicare and Medicaid programs. During a routine internal audit the practice's billing manager discovered that certain claims submitted to and reimbursed by the Medicare and Medicaid programs were "upcoded." The billing manager brings this error to your attention. What are the practice's obligations under state and federal law?

FEDERAL LAW

Liability under the Federal False Claims Act (31 U.S.C. § 3729 et. al).

Reporting and Returning Overpayment (added by the Affordable Care Act):

> "If a person has received an overpayment, the person shall (A) report and return the overpayment to the Secretary, the State, an intermediary, a carrier, or a contractor, as appropriate, at the correct address; and (B) notify the Secretary, State, intermediary, carrier, or contractor to whom the overpayment was returned in writing of the reason for the overpayment." 42 U.S.C. § 1320a-7k(d)

60-day deadline to report and return overpayment: "An overpayment must be reported and returned under paragraph (1) by the later of (A) the date which is 60 days after the date on which the overpayment was identified; or (B) the date any corresponding cost report is due, if applicable." 42 U.S.C. § 1320a-7k(d)

Any overpayment that is retained after the deadline for reporting and returning the overpayment is considered "an obligation" for purposes of the federal False Claims Act liability under 31 U.S.C. § 3729(b)(3).

HYPOTHETICAL #4

You represent a hospital that has a lease rental arrangement with an orthopedic physician's practice. Under the arrangement, the physician pays the hospital a fair market value monthly rent to lease office space from the hospital. The rental agreement expired 8 months ago but the physician has continued to occupy the space and continues to pay the rental amount outlined in the expired agreement. What are the implications under the STARK law?

STARK LAW

The lease exception to the STARK law (42 CFR § 411.357(a)) requires:

- That the agreement be set out in writing, signed by the parties and specifies premises covered;
- The space rented does not exceed those that which is reasonable and necessary for legitimate business purpose of the rental;
- Term must be for at least one year;
- The rental charges over the term of the agreement must be set out in advance;
- The rental charge must not be determined in a way that takes in account the volume or value of referrals or business generated between the parties;
- The agreement must be commercially reasonable even if no referral were made between the parties;
- A month-to-month holdover is allowed for a period of 6 months.

In this hypo, the fact that the lease agreement expired more than 6 months ago means that there is a STARK issue.

- Application of temporary non-compliance provision (42 CFR § 411.353(f)) for arrangements that have fallen out of compliance with STARK. A 90-day period of non-compliance is allowed if [1] the arrangement was in compliance with STARK for at least 180 days prior to when it fell out of compliance; [2] the arrangement has fallen out of compliance for reasons beyond the control of the entity and the entity took prompt steps to rectify the noncompliance; [3] the financial relationship does not violate the Anti-kickback statute or other state/federal regulations.

- STARK Self-Disclosure Protocol (Section 6409, Affordable Care Act).
- Potential violations of the federal and Florida FCAs.
- What if the physician stopped paying rent?

HYPOTHETICAL #5

Your client is a physician practicing with a group practice. Your client's first cousin is a minority owner of a home health agency. Your client and the other physicians in the group refer patients to the cousin's home health agency for care. In addition, your client's wife is a specialty physician who owns an independent practice to which your client and the other physicians in the group refer patients. Are these referral problematic under state and federal law?

FEDERAL LAW

"DHS" and "immediate family" are defined in 42 C.F.R. § 411.351.

- Home health services are DHS but a first cousin is not considered "immediate family" and thus referral are not barred by the STARK law.
- DHS referrals to the wife's practice pose a STARK problem because she is considered immediate family.

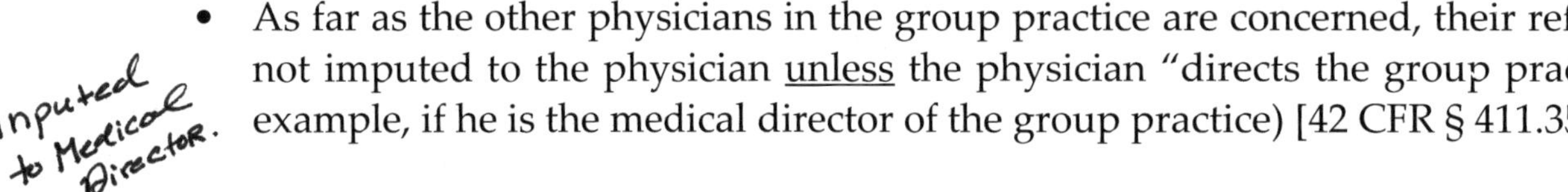

- As far as the other physicians in the group practice are concerned, their referrals are not imputed to the physician unless the physician "directs the group practice" (for example, if he is the medical director of the group practice) [42 CFR § 411.353].

ABOUT THE AUTHORS

Alan S. Gassman is an attorney practicing in Clearwater, Florida with the firm of Gassman Law Associates, P.A. Mr. Gassman's primary practice focus over the past 27 years has been the representation of physicians and their practices as a tax, estate planning and corporate lawyer. Gassman Law Associates, P.A. is a three lawyer firm dedicated to representing physicians, business owners and successful retirees on their personal, professional, and business matters.

Mr. Gassman received his law degree and a post law Masters degree (LL.M.) in Taxation from the University of Florida, and a business degree from Rollins College. He is board certified by The Florida Bar Association in Estate Planning and Trust Law, has the Accredited Estate Planner designation from the National Association of Estate Planners & Councils, and has an AV rating from the Martindale-Hubbell legal directory. He is a commentator for the Leimberg LISI Estate Planning Network, past President of the Pinellas County Estate Planning Council, and has been co-chair and lecturer for two annual Florida Bar Tax Section conferences for over 7 years (Wealth Conservation and Physician Representation).

Mr. Gassman is the lead author of Estate Tax Planning in 2011 and 2012, published by Bloomberg BNA Tax & Accounting, and two other books on physician related topics. He speaks often for national and state sponsored continuing education programs, and has been quoted many times in The Wall Street Journal, Forbes Magazine, Medical Economics, Florida Trend, Florida Medical Business, as well as other well known periodicals. He has published over 150 articles in national and state periodicals on physician, tax, and creditor planning matters.

Lester J. Perling is a Partner in the Fort Lauderdale office of Broad and Cassel. He is a member of the Firm's Health Law and White Collar Civil and Criminal Fraud Defense Practice Groups.

Mr. Perling is a board-certified health law attorney with extensive experience as a health care executive. He holds a master's degree in Health Care Administration. He has had significant experience with Medicare and Medicaid reimbursement and fraud and abuse issues, privacy of health care information (HIPAA), federal and state administrative proceedings, provider operations issues, corporate compliance programs, physician credentialing, transactions between health care providers, and related matters for health care providers.

Mr. Perling had more than 10 years of experience as a health care executive. He held various administrative positions, including Chief Executive Officer, with investor-owned and community hospitals of all types.

Mr. Perling is a member of the Adjunct Faculty at Florida Atlantic University and teaches health law in its Health Care MBA program. Mr. Perling has also taught courses at Florida Atlantic University and Nova Southeastern University, School of Business and Entrepreneurship in provider group practice dynamics, fraud and abuse, and risk management.

He is a frequent national author and lecturer on various health law and health management topics. Mr. Perling's many published works include: "Medicare Claims Appeals Process Handbook," a step by step guide to the appeals process published by Aspen Publishers; "Overview of the Medicare Parts A & B Claims Appeal Process" Chapter in 2009 Medicare and Medicaid Reimbursement Update published by Aspen Publishing and edited by Andrew D. Ruskin; and "Health Care: Whistleblowers Get More Power" article in a June 2009 issue of the National Law Journal.

Mr. Perling was recognized with an AV® Peer Review Rating with Martindale-Hubbell, the agency's highest mark for both competency and ethics and is achieved by only 5 percent of attorneys. Mr. Perling was also designated a "Florida Super Lawyer" by Law & Politics magazine for six consecutive years, recognized in 2006-2012 by Chambers USA: A Guide to America's Leading Business Lawyers in Healthcare, recognized in 2008-2013 by the top legal guide "The Best Lawyers in America," published by Woodward and White and designated a 2009, 2010 and 2011 "Legal Elite" by Florida Trend magazine.

Mr. Perling is Past Chair of The Florida Bar's Health Law Section and Health Law Certification Committee and a member of The Joint Commission's Home Care Professional Technical Advisory Committee.

Kacie Hohnadell, J.D. graduated from Stetson University College of Law in May of 2013 and was the Executive Editor of Stetson Law Review. She received her B.A. from the University of Central Florida in Advertising and Public Relations with a minor in marketing and is an associate attorney with Rodgers-Kiefer Title in Santa Rosa Beach, FL

INDEX

Made in the USA
Middletown, DE
20 March 2016